Twayne's English Authors Series

By Homer T. Cox

UNIVERSITY OF WATERLOO

Henry Seton Merriman

 37

Henry Seton Merriman

By HOMER T. COX

University of Waterloo

Twayne Publishers, Inc.   ::   New York

For Mildred and John, whose encouragement
helped to make it possible

Preface

This study of the life and work of the Late Victorian novelist Henry Seton Merriman has a three-fold objective: (1) to assemble and present the currently available data on Merriman; (2) to examine and evaluate his techniques and ideology in an attempt to demonstrate his importance as an interpreter of the life and thought of his time; and (3) to estimate his place among his contemporaries and his contributions to the art of fiction. For whatever degree of success is evidenced toward the achievement of this goal, the present writer must gratefully acknowledge the help of many hands. Foremost among these is Professor T. E. M. Boll, of the Department of English of the University of Pennsylvania, whose unfailing encouragement and wise counsel made this work possible.

Recognition must also be given to some of the many correspondents in England who have been most helpful. Among these are two cousins of the subject of this study, Mrs. Denise Gibbs and Miss Dorothy Rushton, who were kind enough to furnish certain items of information, letters, and diaries. Merriman's godson, Mr. J. G. Hamilton Jackson, made available photographs and sketches which add interest to the work, Mrs. Olive D'Arcy Hart, a professional researcher, was invaluable in unearthing information which would have been unattainable otherwise, Miss Patricia Butler, of the solicitor's firm of A. P. Watt and Son, Merriman's literary executors, offered much valuable guidance as to sources of information on the novelist.

The present writer would indeed be remiss if he failed to express his genuine appreciation to his wife, Mildred H. Cox, for her patience and tireless efforts in typing the manuscript and assisting with the editing.

Although Henry Seton Merriman's books are out of copyright, special permission has been obtained from Messrs. A. P. Watt and Son, Literary Agents, London, for the many quotations from Merriman's works used in this manuscript. Mrs. Denise Gibbs, who holds copyright to certain of Merriman's letters to his mother and to his unpublished diary, has also graciously given her consent to the use of these materials in direct quotation.

The author is grateful to those journals and magazines still extant for granting the opportunity to use quotations pertaining to Merriman and his work. Many of the periodicals quoted briefly have long since ceased publication. The several correspondents to whom reference is made have authorized quotations from their letters and documents. This includes the letters written by Merriman to William Blackwood and Sons, Limited.

Finally, acknowledgment is made of permission to quote from the books of the following authors and publishers: Cornelius Weygandt, *A Century of the English Novel,* Appleton, Century, Crofts, 1925; Rudyard Kipling, *Kim,* reprinted by permission of Doubleday and Co., Incorporated; Malcolm Elwin, *Old Gods Falling,* William Collins Sons and Co., Limited; Frederic Villiers, *Villiers: His Five Decades of Adventure,* Harper and Row, Publishers; Edward Wagenknecht, *Cavalcade of the English Novel,* Holt, Rinehart and Winston, 1954; *The Illustrated London News,* vol. CXIII; Frank Swinnerton; The London *Times* (Nov. 20, 1903, and Oct. 3, 1957); Lilias Rider Haggard, *The Cloak That I Left,* Hodder and Stoughton; Stanley J. Kunitz and Howard Haycraft, *British Authors of the Nineteenth Century,* H. W. Wilson Co., 1936; Harold Williams, *Modern English Writers: Being a Study of Imaginative Literature, 1890–1914,* 3rd edition, Sidgwick and Jackson, 1925.

HOMER T. COX

University of Waterloo

Contents

Chronology

1862   Henry Seton Merriman (pseudonym of Hugh Stowell Scott) born May 9 at 16 Rye Hill, Elswick, Newcastle-upon-Tyne. Father, Henry, was a shipowner; mother, Mary Sweet Carmichael, was the daughter of the painter James Wilson Carmichael.

1873   Attended Loretta School, Musselburgh, Scotland.

1877   Voyaged to Madras, Calcutta, and Gibraltar aboard his father's ship, the *Tynedale*.

1878   Returned home from voyage.

1880   Joined his father's firm.

1885   Was elected a Member of Lloyd's.

1888   First novel, *Young Mistley*, published anonymously; *The Phantom Future* also published anonymously.

1889   Married, on June 19, Ethel Frances Hall, eldest daughter of the Canon of St. Paul's Cathedral.

1890   Publication of *Suspense*.

1891   Publication of *Prisoners and Captives*.

1892   Publication of *Slave of the Lamp*.

1892   Left the firm of Lloyd's.

1893–   (approximately) Traveled extensively in Europe.
1900

1894   Publication of first major financial and artistic success, *With Edged Tools*.

1895   Identifies himself to his family as a successful novelist, already earning £800 a year.

1900   (approximately) Built a handsome country house near Melton in Suffolk.

1903   Died at Melton on November 19; buried at Eltham, Kent.

1904   Posthumous publication of his last books, *The Last Hope* and *Tomaso's Fortune*.

CHAPTER 1

The "Master of Romance"

IN 1903 there died in England a novelist whose tales captured the popular fancy to such an extent that Frank Swinnerton classed him with A. E. W. Mason and Stanley Weyman as "kings among smaller romantic fry." [1] While the stories of Mason and Weyman are still read fairly widely, those of the third member of Mr. Swinnerton's romantic triumvirate, Hugh Stowell Scott, have been largely forgotten by the present generation; but in his time "he could rely upon loyal readers in sufficient numbers and upon the active interest of editors representing the best of good middle-class taste." That many of Mr. Scott's readers remain loyal is attested by the fact that occasionally a distinguished novelist like Frank Swinnerton or an eminent reviewer like Oliver Edwards of the London *Times* still refers to him.

In his *Times* column, "Talking of Books," October 3, 1957, Mr. Edwards speaks of the "sense of duty" in Hugh Stowell Scott's books as one of the attributes that keep these stories alive after sixty years. Of the fourteen of his volumes selected by Scott himself for survival, Edwards says that these "are an adequate, comprehensive, and durable memorial. They are handy enough to accompany one through life's changes; they have character, and a firm tread, and variety. They do not pall. One or two are indeed weak . . . but there is nothing to disgrace the canon." [2] Many of today's writers would undoubtedly be happy to settle for such a tribute two generations hence.

If Scott's books are neglected by contemporary readers, a part of the blame must devolve upon the author's idiosyncrasies. An extremely modest and retiring man, Scott wrote his first novel anonymously. Thereafter, he used the pseudonym of Henry Seton Merriman because his family disapproved of a writing career. It is possible, too, that his decision to adopt a pseudonym may have resulted from a natural shyness over bearing the same name as the great Sir Walter. So averse was he to publicity of any kind that the books of reference contain little more than the listing and dates of his publications. In his obituary, the *Times* reports that the author would have preferred that there be no notice of his life and works.[3] At his request, no biography was written; he held aloof from interviews during his lifetime; he refused to take part in literary society; and, except for Stanley Weyman, he made no intimate literary friends. He believed a writer should be known to the public only by his books. Concerning these peculiarities Malcolm Elwin says: "Biography supplies an illuminating complement to criticism, and the artist who hides his personality from scrutiny must expect the critics to ignore him."[4] Tracing the facts in the career of so reticent a man is an interesting, if frequently frustrating, problem in detection.

Hugh Stowell Scott—or, as he insisted on being known, Henry Seton Merriman—was born on May 9, 1862, at 16 Rye Hill, Elswick, Newcastle-upon-Tyne. His father, Henry Scott, was a shipowner; his mother, the former Mary Sweet Carmichael, was the daughter of James Wilson Carmichael, a marine painter.[5] According to a letter[6] received from Hugh's cousin, Mrs. Denise Gibbs, the elder Mr. Scott was a man "very gentle and greatly loved." An enclosed notice printed at the time of Mr. Scott's death at age sixty-five reveals that the businessman and Tyneside merchant had many other facets to his nature. He was a director of *The Graphic* and the *Daily Graphic,* as well as of the company that built the galleries of the Royal Institute of Painters in Water Colors. Thus young Hugh inherited artistic inclinations from both his father and mother. Concerning Hugh's mother, Mrs. Gibbs describes her great-aunt Mary Scott as an "extremely strong-minded, clever woman, ruling her family (often much against their will), but she was certainly a clever woman."[7] Judging from his later action, it is interesting to speculate that Hugh may have had other ideas about the ruling member of the family, for it was not until after his father's death in 1895 that he wrote a letter to his mother revealing for the first time that he was the successful novelist Henry Seton Merriman.[8]

It was probably the artist and war correspondent Frederic Villiers[9] who was responsible for a possibly apocryphal anecdote

about Hugh's relationship with his father. Villiers had occasion
to stay at the home of the elder Scott in 1877, when Hugh was
fifteen years old. He found the embryo romancer "a fair youth,"
retiring and secretive. The boy remained much at home because
he was considered delicate. He was absorbed in literary studies
while his older brother, Henry Carmichael Scott, went daily to
business in the city. Hugh's father apparently came to resent the
fact that the young man stayed away from business with the
excuse of writing while his brother Harry worked. He would
often ask Hugh when he intended to drop this literary folly and
join his brother in the family business. Some years later, according to Villiers, Mr. Scott showed his son a book, *The Sowers,*
which he had just purchased at a bookstall. "Now if you could
produce a book like this," said Mr. Scott, "you might call your-
self a writer."

The story has been repeated with slight variations by several
of Merriman's relatives and contemporaries. Frank Swinnerton
mentions it without citing the book in question.[10] The Reverend
G. Williams[11] recounts the tale, using Merriman's first published
work, *Young Mistley,* as the illustrative volume. Old wives' tale
or not, Mr. Villiers must have been wrong about the novel in
question; *The Sowers,* Merriman's greatest popular success, was
not published until 1896, about a year after Mr. Scott's death.

If Hugh gave his father some anxious moments, his older
brother Henry apparently performed quite satisfactorily his filial
duties. After serving in his father's ship and insurance brokerage
firm, Henry became a member of the firm of Lloyd's of London
in 1884.[12] Hugh also joined the firm of Henry Scott and Sons,
at the age of eighteen,[13] and became associated with Lloyd's in
1885; he remained with his father's firm until 1892, when he gave
up business permanently for literature.[14] Hugh had another
brother who is not identified by name or age in any of the references, and an apparently younger and favorite sister, Eva Russell
Scott, who, along with Henry, is remembered generously in
Hugh's will. These four children completed the family.

Hugh was formally educated, albeit somewhat sketchily, at
Loretto School, Musselburgh, Scotland, and at Vevey, Switzer-
land, and Wiesbaden, Germany.[15] The schools at Vevey and
Wiesbaden are not named, but the current Headmaster at Loretto

School writes that his school register lists only the fact that Hugh Stowell Scott attended Loretto School from October to December, 1873.[16] Since he apparently attended the school only three months, it is not surprising that details are lacking. In view of the social and economic prominence of his family, such institutional training was possibly supplemented by private tutors.

In 1877, at the age of fifteen, the boy made a voyage to Madras, Calcutta, Ceylon, Aden, Malta, Gibraltar, and returned to Southampton in his father's sailing ship, the *Tynedale*. Fortunately he kept a log of this trip in which we can discern some evidence of the widespread interests and observational powers of the budding novelist.[17] Although much of the text of the diary is occupied with the routine minutiae of daily shipboard life, there are occasional passages that reveal such of the lad's hobbies as painting, drawing, writing, and model building; his love for his family; his interest in new places and people; some latent narrative and descriptive power; and the traditional English fondness for hunting and other adventuring. Frequent references to attacks of biliousness confirm Mr. Villiers' diagnosis of frail health.

On Sunday, November 11, Hugh records nostalgically that "it is mama's birthday, but I cannot wish her many happy returns even by letter. It is," he adds plaintively, "about the most un-Sundaylike Sunday I have ever spent." He frequently reports progress on a boat model that he is building, the drawing and fretwork that he is doing, and the writing of his own past history. Accounts of gamebird shooting, both aboard ship and ashore, and visits to church services, the theater, and the opera when the ship is in port attest to his reflection of the upper middle-class concern in the later Victorian era with sport, culture, and religion.

The passage describing his first Christmas at sea demonstrates the developing power for writing with economy and restraint that may be observed in the later novelist:

Tuesday, 25th—Christmas Day. The first, and perhaps the last Christmas day I shall spend at sea. I got up pretty early and went on deck, but there were no birds; when I came downstairs to the cabin to breakfast I was surprised to see some neat little packets addressed in Nan's well-known writing. I hurried to open them, and found a present from each one of the family. Of course I was pleased, but it made me feel a little sad to think how many miles I was away from them. I know they will be thinking of me today, and wondering where I am, but I hope that the steamer which we spoke to will have arrived by this time, and let them know that we are all well. After breakfast the Captain loaded the old rifle for me and I went on deck to try a shot, the first I have ever fired. A bird came near, and I fired, but of course missed. I tried a second shot and missed again, but I hit my third try, but only wounded the bird.

It was nearly dinner time by this time, so I went to set fire to the plum puddings. We had dinner, quite a Christmas dinner. We had killed one of the fowls and made broth of it and then ate it. After dinner I took the gun on deck again. This time I was more lucky. My first three shots I killed the bird each time, and wounded the fourth, but my shots were limited. I did not shoot any more. The ship was rolling tremendously, and the birds were on the wing, so it was very good shooting for a beginner. Later in the afternoon it fell a calm, so we began fishing for albatross. We caught two large ones, the biggest measuring 10 ft. 6 in. from the tip of one wing, to the tip of the other. Their beaks were seven inches long. The birds that I shot were marloss and measure about 7 ft. from tip to tip.

After having had some hot port wine and water to drink the health of those at home, we turned in, and thus ended the most strangely spent Christmas day that I remember out of all my fifteen.

Occasional passages devoted to recording incidents of the voyage reveal a talent for adroit selection of details in a narrative as well as a keen sense of humor, although the whole is somewhat spoiled by the diarist's evident impatience with the act of writing. The entry for June 7, 1878, especially, is full of a boyish exuberance and love of fun:

Friday, 7th—We got moored alongside the quay by daybreak. Went up to town of Suez (4 miles) in a boat with Mr. Cheetham, Renny, Martin, and Swart. We were punted, the men running along the gunwale, but one of them slipped and fell in, much to our delight. Renny and I got a donkey each, and went to the bazaars, and bought a few things. Then we galloped back to tiffin on board, and both enjoyed our ride. My donkey was called Sir Roger. Renny's Old Obadiah. We spent the rest of the day quietly on board. Went for a walk in the evening. I was surprised and delighted to find a letter from home had come for me.

Still another entry for the same year shows the lad's fine sensitivity and strong family attachment:

Thursday, 9th—My birthday [his sixteenth]. I know they will be thinking of me at home today. I wish we were on the passage home, and out of this miserable Bay of Bengal. I am looking forward to getting letters when we get to Madras. Nobody on board knows it is my birthday, and I am not going to tell them. It is no good.

Notice that in spite of his heartache, young Hugh is already emulating the stoical and uncommunicative characters of his later novels. At whatever cost, he suppresses his sentiments. Even though it is "no good," nobody shall know of his homesickness.

An earlier passage is fairly typical of the several descriptive passages scattered through the diary. As he was to do later in his novels, Hugh wrote rapidly and straightforwardly. Always more interested in the total impression than in minutiae, the boy found it necessary, even as the man did later, to convey his description, at least in part, through people and stirring action. The result, as in this early example, is often a characterization of a place rather than a detailed description:

Tuesday, 30th—Went ashore in longboat with pilot and Captain. Went to shipping agency and then had a look through Ryde, a very pretty town, but we felt rather shabby as we had not dressed much. Went across to Portsmouth by Princess of Wales. Had a look round and dined in a very dirty eating house. Bought a few things. We were disappointed in the town, dirty straggly place, full of untidy soldiers and sailors, not nearly such a nice place as Ryde. The wind began to get up about two o'clock. Went back to Ryde and went to postoffice, but no return telegrams had arrived. Longboat had put out, but only manned by a very weak crew with the 2nd mate. They could not make the land as tide and wind were against them. They drifted away to the leeward, and ran foul of a Norwegian brig to which they made fast. Have left them to their fate as it is no good sending for them tonight as it is very heavy boat. They will have to stay on the brig all night. We came aboard in a shore boat which brought us over at a good rate as the wind is high.

The passage above alters perceptibly in fluidity of expression when the boy begins to write about the sea. Although he cared little for the prosaic details of his father's business, the romantic aspects of it are here revealed as a very real part of his heritage. Such a passage clearly presages Hugh's lifelong love of travel and adventure in various parts of the globe—a love that may very well have received its impetus during this early ten months' voyage on his father's ship.

Only one other item remains to be discussed in connection with this diary. On the last page of the ledger in which the diary is kept, several blank pages removed from the last page of text of the log itself, appears a poem in Hugh's handwriting, each line of which is enclosed in quotation marks. The saccharine sentimentality of the verse is of a type which appeared frequently in Guest Books of the later Victorian era. Since no clue is available as to its authorship, to the occasion for its writing, or to the inspiration for its subject matter, it is useless to speculate upon the origins of the poem. The extravagant and hackneyed phraseology of its imagery would certainly make it attributable to a youthful swain, as would the unsophisticated attitude toward womankind found in the piece. Despite its cloying figures, the poem expresses quite clearly the noble and protective attitude of the Victorian male toward silent and suffering woman. If the poem was in fact Hugh's own, it prefigures the typical Merriman heroine; if it is simply a poem which he admired and copied out from some other source, it may serve as an early clue to the formation of his limited concept of the psychology of the female.

In July, 1878, after a voyage of ten months, Hugh returned home, having visited many of the places which he was to revisit often in later life; some of them were to become the backgrounds for his tales of high romance. The period between 1878 and 1885 must have been a restless sort of time during which young Hugh was trying to find himself. The idea of a business career was then, as also later, distasteful to him. The fact that in this interim his older brother Harry dutifully recognized his responsibility by joining the firm aroused no emulatory response in Hugh. We have Mr. Villiers' word [18] that the boy continued his writing in secret and that this activity was apparently the cause of some family friction.

According to a letter from Joseph Spurr, an associate of Hugh's at Lloyd's, the young man eventually accepted a post in an East

Indian merchant's office for a few months and then returned to
England to join this company's office in London. Meanwhile, the
firm of Henry Scott and Sons had been commissioned in 1883
as ship and insurance brokers at Lloyd's.[19] After serving in his
father's firm, Henry became a Member of Lloyd's of London in
1884. As indicated above, Hugh also joined the firm of Henry
Scott and Sons, at the age of eighteen, and was elected a Member of Lloyd's in 1885.[20]

It must have been at about this time that Hugh and his brother
Harry made a trip to Rome. In two letters which have been
made available[21] the young Hugh chats very entertainingly with
his mother about his activities in that city. The letters reveal a
considerable improvement, both in literary style and in power
of observation, over the diary of his first voyage, written approximately ten years earlier. The letters show adroitness in carica-
turing people in a line or two. There is Mrs. Russel, for instance,
who goes in for "archaeological lectures and a-improving of her
mind," or Mr. Reginald Soames "dreaming in front of the Gladiator with his mouth open." The lines about "neat" little Miss Gay
also show his nice touch, but best of all is the comedy of errors
concerning the stupid Mr. Hayes' well-intentioned but erroneous
disquisition on art. Brief as they are, these sketches suggest the
bent toward gentle satire that was to figure rather largely in the
later novels:

Rome
Sunday, 26th Feb.

Dearest Mother, Papa and Eva

We have just got mother and Eva's [his sister] letters for which we
are much obliged, you will be spoiling us, this is the second letter in
two days. I wonder what Papa thought of Spezzia, we did not see
much of it as we passed. We determined to do a little sight-seeing this
morning and go to church in the afternoon, as so many of the Museums
and Galleries are free on Sunday and not in the week; we went to the
Capitol where there are some beautiful and well-known statues of the
Dying Gladiator, etc. From there we went to the Palazzo dei Conserv-
atori (opposite the Capitol) where there are some very good pictures
and we went just behind the Palace and saw the Tarpeian Rock, and
then we went to the Palatine Hill of the Palace of the Caesars where
all the Roman aristocracy used to live and then we came back very

late for lunch; after lunch we called in to a small museum on our way to church; it was not much of a museum and its only recommendation is that it is free on Sundays. The service is held in a large sort of Hall until the church is built. We had a very good sermon. We were surprised at the amount of English people in the Galleries, etc. this morning, and expected the church to be full this afternoon, but it was not. I am afraid Rome is an unhealthy place for people's minds and morals as well as for their bodies, as it induces them to give up church for pecuniary reasons. We must have saved about 7 liras this morning, but then we went to church this afternoon and put 50 centimes in the plate. We saw Mr. Reginald Soames in the Capitol "dreaming" in front of the Gladiator with his mouth open. At church we saw Miss West and in the Pincio the two men belonging to the broken legged party at Alassio.

We have not seen Mr. Milligan yet; Mrs. Russel is not the sort of woman I expected; she is tall and thin with rather an anxious look and quite white hair. She is going in for attending archaeological lectures and a-improving of her mind. Her mother was there, a nice looking old body. If Eva wants some more socks to practice on, she has just to say so, and we will send off a packet by post.

> With best love,
> Believe me
> Your loving son,
> Hugh S. Scott

Rome, 3rd March

Dearest Mother:

We have had no letter from you since that enclosing Mr. Jackson's, but I dare say to-day's second post will bring one.

We had a very nice walk yesterday afternoon and saw several interesting places. Mr. Milligan is a very nice fellow and a very instructive guide. Last night we had a severe thunderstorm. Harry and I went to a place where we got a good view of the town to watch the lightening [*sic*]; it was beautiful. As we got rather wet in coming back we thought we would go to bed at once, but Mr. Hayes turned up just before Harry began undressing; as I was already in bed Harry went down and saw the old gentleman; he had come to arrange about meeting this morning and going to the Borghese Gallery and some churches so we went to their Pension this morning. We were at once pounced upon by the Misses Christie who were extremely gushing and sent their kind regards to you. Mr. Hayes is a little more stupid than ever, giving a long and glowing account of some picture and its painter then being gently informed by Mrs. Hayes that it is the wrong painter and wrong picture and that the story was not quite correct generally. Miss Gay goes trotting about with her neat little shawl and neat little guide book and looking at everything in a neat little way. She is getting quite fat and talks to everybody, goes into long rambling stories of unheard of saints with monks who show people through the churches, and got into conversation with several of the artists copying pictures in the Borghese; in fact I think the sooner she gets back to Alassio the better. Mrs. Hayes is astonished and very satisfied with the manner in which we have been seeing Rome and the amount we have done. We are to meet again this afternoon and go to see the Quirinal Palace, which is where the king and queen are living.

6 P.M.

We have just come in and found your letter waiting for us. I don't know how it is that you did not get a letter from us as we have posted a letter or card every day regularly. I dare say you would get two the following day. You must be very glad to get away from the Bubs & Co. Mr. Hayes told me he had heard from a great many people that Mr. Bub quite spoilt their enjoyment. We leave for Naples at 6 on Monday morning, Harry told you in one of his letters, but it may not have reached you. We note what Papa says on his slip, we saw Lake Krasymene [sic] in coming, the train runs a good way round it, but it takes 5 hours by train from Rome.

There are so many places to go out of Rome that we are not going to any, Tivoli, Ostia, Trascali, etc. etc. and besides we have our time quite filled up with Rome itself, several people in the hotel have been on nearly all the excursions and come back very tired and not enthusiastic at all. This afternoon we went to the King's Palace with the Hayes, then back to their Pension and had tea in their bedroom out of tumblers; then Harry and I left and went to the Pamphili-Doria Villa which has beautiful grounds.

We are both quite well, but still troubled with fearful appetites though we always get quite enough at meals.

Your loving son,
Hugh S. Scott

By this time, certainly, the first novel must have been well along. That the novelist was learning his trade is quite apparent in the foregoing letters. This novel, *Young Mistley*, was published anonymously in 1888. The young writer was not yet ready to acknowledge his offspring. He still had to prove to himself, to the world, and, still more important, to his family, that he was truly a writer before he dared to take the long step from the world of business to that of literature. There was, after all, the very real fact of his father's disapproval, one no less severe because of that father's own literary leanings. In fact, the elder Scott's recognition of such inclinations in himself probably dictated his severity toward his son's aspirations.

Doubtless beginning by this time to feel somewhat surer of his writing vocation, Hugh married, on June 19, 1889, Ethel Frances Hall,[22] the eldest daughter of Canon Hall of St. Paul's Cathedral.[23] Judging from her photograph,[24] Miss Hall was a young woman of great personal beauty and charm. None of the available correspondence gives any insight into the character of Hugh's wife. Ada M. Orpen, who lived near the novelist's last home at Melton some years after his death, writes in *John O'London's Weekly,* in response to the article by Frank Swinnerton mentioned previously, that "His [Scott's] wife put up a beautiful little window in the church to his memory. She was also an outstanding personality and greatly loved by all." [25] Mr. Hamilton Jackson mentions the young Mrs. Scott simply as his godmother, but of Hugh he speaks quite fondly, despite the fact that the novelist died when this godson was only four years old.[26] His widow survived him without issue; in August, 1912, nine years after his death, she married the Reverend George Augustus Cobbold, perpetual curate of St. Bartholomew's, Ipswich.[27]

Hugh's marriage was, however, fortunate for the writer. Through his wife he became associated with her sister, Evelyn Beatrice Hall. Miss Hall, herself a writer under the pseudonym of S. G. Tallentyre, became not only his lifelong friend and occasional collaborator, but also his most enthusiastic aider and abettor in his pursuit of a writing career. It may have been she— presuming that he knew her prior to his marriage—who, as Ada Orpen says,[28] started Merriman on the road to literary success. Certainly, she, together with James Payn,[29] a long-time friend, gave him every encouragement to persevere. Furthermore, she and Hugh's wife edited and issued a Memorial Edition of Merriman's work in fourteen volumes in 1909–1910.[30]

Miss Hall, or Stephen G. Tallentyre, as she preferred to be known professionally, wrote several books of her own in addition to those on which she collaborated with her more famous brother-in-law. Among her works was a lengthy *Life of Voltaire* and two novels, *Matthew Hargraves* and *Early Victorian*.[31] With her death in April, 1956, intimate information about Merriman was lost. The only Merriman memorabilia among her effects were the diary and letters left to Mrs. Gibbs that we have previously discussed.

Concerning Evelyn Hall, Miss Dorothy Rushton, Hugh's cousin by marriage, says that she and Merriman "were great assets to any form of charades and acting." [32] Miss Rushton saw Hugh often during these years, especially during the Christmas holidays when the clan gathered at Brecon House, Eltham, the home of Hugh's father-in-law. She describes him as a "Yachting enthusiast, very tall, well over six feet and [he] wore his hair *à la brosse*, which certainly gave him a foreign appearance. He spoke French perfectly, and as far as I can remember some German and had travelled in all the countries of the setting of his novels. . . ." [33]

To this portrait of Scott at home might be added Miss Hall's account of the author abroad, one that gives some insight into his working methods of acquiring background and atmosphere for his novels: "His greatest delight was to merge himself completely in the life and interests of the country he was visiting—to stay at the mean *venta* or the *auberge* where the tourist was never seen—to sit in the local cafes of an evening and listen to local politics and gossip; to read for the time nothing but the native newspapers, and no literature but the literature, past and present, of the land where he was sojourning." [34]

Once started, the novels were published in fairly rapid succession. The anonymous *Young Mistley* was followed, again in 1888, by *The Phantom Future*, the first book to be signed with the pen name of Henry Seton Merriman. In 1890 came *Suspense*, and in 1891, *Prisoners and Captives*. With the publication of *The Slave of the Lamp* in 1892, Merriman came to a turning point in his life. Despite the fact that he considered his first four books "crude and immature" and later withdrew them from publication,[35] Merriman had been well enough received, both by critic and public, to feel that he could safely withdraw from business altogether. Accordingly, he left Lloyd's in 1892, never to return.

Thereafter, he traveled widely, usually with his wife or with his fellow romanticist, Stanley J. Weyman.[36]

Although Hugh's income was growing along with his fame as a novelist, he continued to conceal the identity of Henry Seton Merriman from his family. Not until after his first major financial and artistic success, *With Edged Tools*, in 1894—and incidentally after his father's death—did he nerve himself to the point of admitting to his mother that he was Henry Seton Merriman. In a letter written from France on June 7, 1895, and previously referred to, Hugh reveals his struggles to learn the craft of the novelist, his present success with the publishers and the periodicals, and his hopes for the future. The letter makes clear what would have been very difficult to conceal: the fact that his wife had known of his literary activities since the beginning of their marriage. It also reveals the rather impressive fact that his income from writing, after only seven years of effort, was already £800 a year. A reference to his sister Eva, who according to Miss Rushton has been dead "some years," [37] indicated that Eva had already succumbed to the spell of Merriman's fancy without being aware that her favorite author was her brother.

Of particular interest in respect to this study is Merriman's stated determination, and one often repeated, to avoid sedulously the "honour and glory" of authorship and his resolve to retain his literary alias in order to "lead a quiet and obscure life" devoid of "humbug." These resolutions he studiously kept for the eight years of life remaining to him.

We have Mr. Villiers' word that the revelation of Merriman's true identity did not pass without some ironic repercussions among his family. "When at last," Mr. Villiers writes, "his people found out that he was the most popular writer of the day . . . his people, instead of being supremely proud of him, raised a howl of indignation because he had been receiving big fees without letting anyone know of his good fortune. They had embittered him by ridiculing his early struggle for literary fame." [38] If Villiers' accusation is true, the family reaction to his revelation must have convinced Merriman even more firmly that he had been right in seeking to preserve his anonymity as long as possible.

Internal evidence within the novels, coupled with Merriman's rigorous determination to avoid all public notice, suggests that the novelist might have been engaged in his later years in some sort of intelligence activity for the British government. As will be pointed out later in detail, many of his books deal with the adventures of secret-service agents. His passionate and almost constant devotion to travel, from the time he left Lloyd's until his death, would certainly have given him ample opportunity for this sort of endeavor. Such an activity, too, would make more understandable his nearly pathologic refusal to allow the publication of any biographical material. The Reverend G. Williams[39] quotes an unidentified correspondent on the fact of Merriman's reluctance to identify himself publicly. Villiers[40] and Elwin[41] also make a point of Merriman's refusal to divulge personal details, as do Kunitz and Haycraft[42] and the editors of the *Dictionary of National Biography*.[43]

The few members of the novelist's family and associates who are still living are no less unanimous in their recognition of his reticence. Miss Rushton[44] and Mrs. Gibbs[45] comment on it, and Mr. Hamilton Jackson[46] and Mr. Spurr[47] note his silence concerning personal activities. These people, however, are inclined to attribute Merriman's attitude to early family conditioning and criticism in respect to a writing career rather than to reticence for official reasons. Hamilton Jackson feels "quite sure that he [Merriman] was not employed in any form of intelligence or secret service." Merriman's extensive traveling is ascribed by Hamilton Jackson to the fact that "he felt very strongly that an author should have first hand knowledge of the localities in his books." Miss Rushton states that "not to my knowledge was he [Merriman] ever employed in any secret service activity." Mr. Spurr declared categorically that "You may be quite sure that he had nothing to do with espionage or intrigue of any kind whatever." Like Hamilton Jackson, Spurr attributes Merriman's numerous tours simply to an inordinate love for the foreign scene and to a desire to lend verisimilitude to his settings.

Letters to the British Consular Service in this country and to the United States Consulate in England were answered by referral to the British Information Services in Washington, D.C. Their reply was an emphatic assurance that "There is no way in which the records of British Intelligence Services can be searched; all matters pertaining to these Services remain strictly secret." [48] Mrs. Olive S. D'Arcy Hart, a professional researcher working in London, met with no better success in applying to His Majesty's Treasury Service.[49] Despite the fact that no definitive answer will probably be obtainable, the question of Scott's putative connection with secret-service activity is an interesting one with respect both to England's involvement in the uneasy international relationships incident to the expansion of her empire and to the overriding concern with such matters exhibited in the author's published work.

Some time near the turn of the century, Merriman returned to England, having made good use of his travel experiences, with the apparent intention of settling down. He built the handsome house, Long Spring,[50] near Melton, Woodbridge, Suffolk,[51] about twelve miles from Ipswich.

Merriman, at this time on the very crest of success, must have been looking forward to a more leisurely pursuit of his writing career. In the space of fourteen years, he had published a volume of essays, a book of character sketches, and seventeen novels, including *The Sowers*, which ran to thirty editions in England alone and was reprinted by Tauchnitz in Germany.[52] Editors, whether of publishing houses or of the better magazines, were ready to publish anything he wrote.[53] Many of his novels were first serialized in such upper middle-class journals as the *Cornhill* and *Windsor*.

In 1903 two more of his works, a novel entitled *The Last Hope* and a collection of his short stories called *Tomaso's Fortune*, had been finished but were to be published posthumously the following year. At the age of forty-one, after living in his handsome new home only eighteen months, Merriman died on November 19, 1903, of an appendicitis abscess collapse.[54] He was buried at Eltham, Kent.[55]

Scott's will,[56] originally made out in 1896, was that of a man of considerable substance and acumen. To his sister-in-law and collaborator, Evelyn Beatrice Hall, he left the sum of £4000, clear, "in token of my gratitude for her continued assistance and literary advice without which I should never have been able to have made a living by my pen." A later codicil, written the day before he died, increased this bequest to £5000. The balance of his estate, minus a few small bequests, was left to his wife in trust for any children who might be born. There followed some details as to the manner in which his estate should be liquidated, and the naming of his brother, Henry, and his brother-in-law, Arthur Gwynne Hall, as executors and trustees. A first codicil, written in 1901, removed his brother-in-law as trustee in favor of his sister, Eva. The final codicil, previously mentioned, provided for his wife an income of £1000 annually, since there were no children, and left anything accruing above this sum to his brother and sister in the proportion of two-thirds to Henry and one-third to Eva.

Of those mentioned in the will who have not already been accounted for, Miss Rushton has written to Mrs. D'Arcy Hart that she thinks "the brother Harry [Henry] Scott died many years ago." This fact has been confirmed by the literary agents Messrs. A. P. Watts. Miss Rushton states further that "the brother-in-law, Arthur Gwynne Hall, died in 1940 in Scotland where he lived . . . his sister-in-law, Norah Hall, died in Tunbridge Wells in 1926." [57]

There is little that can be added to the portrait of Hugh Stowell Scott, a man who concealed his private life to the very end under the shadow of Henry Seton Merriman, but one whose literary star led him to transient fame and considerable fortune. All his reviewers admit his rare skill as a story-teller; but, because of the scantiness of available materials, there has not yet been an attempt to assess his total contribution as a writer. Perhaps he has been overlooked since his death because his sheer virtuosity as a teller of tales has beguiled the reader from seeing beyond the romantic adventurer.

Yet Merriman has by no means been entirely forgotten. As was mentioned earlier, a collected edition of his work was issued in 1910. The London *Evening News* for September 22, 1931, stated that the last four of his novels were to be reprinted shortly by the firm of John Murray. According to Mrs. D'Arcy Hart, the British Broadcasting Corporation produced, some time ago, a serialized version of one of his later novels, *Barlasch of the Guard*.[58] There have been several recent journal and newspaper articles referring to Merriman and his work, among them those by Frank Swinnerton and Oliver Edwards, previously quoted. Finally, the Messrs. Maggs Brothers, London booksellers, advertised for sale, not long ago, some of Merriman's letters and manuscript papers. Among these items were a few manuscript pages of what the bookseller described as an unpublished novel, *The Great Game*.[59] Unfortunately, if it was in fact a novel, the rest of the manuscript is apparently lost. While all this information is scarcely enough evidence to indicate a true revival of interest, it does show that Merriman is still remembered with fondness and respect, after sixty years. There must be a reason for this reaction, therefore, beyond his ability to spin a plot. This study seeks to discover that reason.

CHAPTER 2

Trial Balloons

IN 1888, while still ostensibly employed at Lloyd's, Scott published his first novel. It was entitled *Young Mistley* and was issued anonymously by Smith, Elder and Company in two volumes. It was followed in the same year by *The Phantom Future*, also in two volumes, and in 1890 and 1891, by *Suspense* and *Prisoners and Captives* respectively, each in three volumes. The three last novels were signed with the *nom de plume* which he employed for each of his successive novels.

Since this remarkable productivity established the pattern for his entire career as a writer, it is not strange that Henry Seton Merriman soon became a name thoroughly familiar to readers of the late Victorian era. The only thing unusual in the situation is that Merriman could sustain this writing pace over a period of four or five years and still make even a pretense of carrying on a regular occupation. Had he not used ill health "as a plea for neglecting business," [1] he would certainly have had to withdraw from active participation in business much earlier. That he was able to achieve a popularity, meanwhile, that led him to decide in four short years to terminate his regular employment is, in itself, a tribute to his storytelling gifts.[2]

A rereading of the first four books persuaded Merriman that they were "crude and immature," and he decided to withdraw them. He found, however, that he could not prevent their being reprinted in America and elsewhere; consequently, he rewrote them, though "conscious of a hundred defects which the most careful revision cannot eliminate." These four, along with *Dross*, first published as a serial but not issued as a book until 1899 because it fell below his standard, were later added to the collected edition of his works.[3]

I Young Mistley

Foreshadowing virtually all of Merriman's succeeding novels, the action of *Young Mistley* ranges back and forth among a number of diverse and widely separated locales. The plot also shows a pattern which is common to most of Merriman's novels. A man and a woman of the upper middle class are brought together. The man is either already, or he becomes, engaged in a potentially dangerous task. Various complications are introduced which temporarily forestall a declaration of mutual love. The hero and heroine are contrasted against other couples in a somewhat similar situation. Several people of mysterious origin whose motives are obscure are introduced in order to augment suspense. Chance or some tragic fault within themselves causes one or more of these men and women to react inimically to the forces of good. Through perseverance and personal sacrifice, the values represented by the hero and heroine are eventually triumphant, but the culmination is not always a happy one. It might be argued that the plot situation outlined above is a fairly close approximation to life. To the extent that it is, Merriman is a realistic writer. Since he often permits chance or fate to affect results, however, the author's method places him in the realm of melodrama.

This book also allows the author, through his major characters, to explore two of his favorite themes: Charles, Winyard, and the Colonel illustrate the importance of self-reliance in their single-minded devotion to duty; and Laurance Lowe and Lena, as well as Winyard and Charles, are expressions of the self-sacrifice of which genuine love is capable. Winyard, Charles, and the Colonel make whatever denials are necessary in order to pursue the honorable path of duty. Laurance has sublimated his love for Mrs. Wright into a passionate and stoical devotion to her family; Lena risks her health and her social position in a sincere but futile attempt to aid the man she loves; Charles conceals his own feelings for Lena when he recognizes her obvious preference for his brother; and Winyard endures a great danger and hardship, impelled, at least in part, by a desire to prove himself in the eyes of Lena and her family before he declares his love.

Many of the people in this and the succeeding novels are a part of the upper middle-class milieu in which Merriman moved. The pervasive air of ease and luxury in the book is that of the author's wealthy, shipowning family. There can be little doubt that Winyard is an idealized projection of his creator. Merriman's love of travel and adventure is echoed in Winyard. The amateur theatricals described in the book recall Miss Rushton's memories of her cousin's fondness for such activity. Hints of Merriman's feeling toward his family are to be found in Winyard's attitude toward the Colonel and Mrs. Wright, Charles and Mrs. Mistley.

The social values implicit in the story are identical with those in the author's social environment. The patriarchal nature of his family and the sacredness of family ties are exemplified by the Wrights and the Mistleys in their various interrelationships. The subordinate social position of woman in that period is emphasized by Mrs. Wright's self-effacing devotion to her husband and by that of Mrs. Mistley to her sons. It is significant, too, that such characters as Monsieur Jacobi, Ivan Meyer, and Marie Bakovitch, whose activities are something less than admirable, are foreign rather than English. Merriman dramatically implies that the Englishman was naturally honest in pursuing his superior course in life, and that he must bear the "white man's burden" as he goes about the world bringing right and order to undeveloped areas and to the underprivileged peoples who inhabit them.

Stylistically, the book is derivative, both in its narrative techniques and in its use of language. Many of these stylistic devices were used consistently by the author throughout his work. Elwin points out that "the influences for the writing of *Young Mistley* were obviously French; Merriman went directly to Flaubert, de Maupassant, and de Goncourt, without passing, like George Moore, through a phase of devotion to the naturalism of Zola." [4] Wagenknecht reiterates this French influence.[5]

Mistley shows the loose construction to be expected from a beginning novelist, but Elwin finds in it also " a striving for cohesion, for rejection of all elements superfluous to the plot, which amounted almost to innovation as early as 1888. This cohesion, simplicity and shapeliness of design, which has become the first principle of the modern novel, is clearly Merriman's primary objective, and his success in its achievement marks him as a pioneer in the novel's transition from Victorian shapelessness to modern conformity." [6]

Contemporary reviewers were not so generous in their response to Merriman's maiden effort. Their reaction was in general agreement with the reviewer for *The Academy,* who praises the introduction of intrigue in the novel but concludes primarily that the author "lacks the technique for this sort of thing." [7]

Merriman's characterizations are especially weak in this novel. The people are hurried on and off stage much in the manner of puppets, who act not as the result of forces from within themselves but in response to external manipulation. For this reason they are apt to be "flat" rather than "round"—single rather than multifaceted. The incidents in which they take part, moreover, are managed much like the scenes in a play. Each one starts in a relatively low key and rises, through a series of complications, to a little climax of suspense. The skill with which the author shifts back and forth from one of these scenes to another, as well as his ability to weave them together eventually into a cohesive plot, indicates that Merriman might have been an equally successful writer for the stage. This theatricality tends to move Merriman's work farther from the world of reality toward the domain of melodrama.

Just as the author's heroes are models for gentlemanly conduct, his heroines are paragons of female behavior. Even the "bad" or self-seeking girls who invariably turn up in his novels are never wholly so. They conform to the code of respectability and seldom do anything worse than marry for money, or they may be led astray from a mistaken sense of duty, like Marie in *Young Mistley.* In their associations with men, they strictly observe the proprieties. Marie and Ivan are in love and, for a time, they live together in a common suite of rooms; but their association, until the time of their marriage, is like that of a brother and sister. The wholly admirable girls, like Lena Wright, have beauty, patience, nerve, and endurance. While they often tactfully conceal their love, as Lena does, they accept without coquetry proposals of marriage from the men they love.

These people, both men and women, lack depth because they are *in* life but not *of* it. They accept stoically whatever fate has in store for them, but they neither grow nor deteriorate through experience. They are fixed forever in an epoch of time like the figures in Keats's "Ode on a Grecian Urn." That epoch is the British world of the 1860's and 1870's, which is for the author an earlier and happier time, wherein people in comfortable economic circumstances moved quietly and easily from the serenity of the country estate or the smart London suburb to scenes of occasional violence abroad. Often, these people work; but their work is done not so much to gain a livelihood as to accept the alluring challenge of adventure or intrigue. This situation is certainly a reflection of some of the ideas of the era's rapidly rising middle class. Yet the author has no affinity either for the get-rich-quick "carpet knights" or for the aesthetes and intellectuals of his own time who dissipate their energies in pursuit of artistic or philosophical chimeras; his concern is rather with men "who love fighting for its own sake, and not only for the gain of it." [8]

The introduction of the nihilistic theme in *Young Mistley* reinforces the impression that the author was a convinced advocate of Britain's policy of paternalistic imperialism, and it also confirms his interest in what might be described as "the Russian question." Many of his later novels exploit the Russian scene, and particularly British interest in the containment of Russia and in the liberation of the Russian peasant from the persecution of the Czarist regime. Merriman's understanding of the unrest in Europe and the Near East sometimes gave rise to asides of prophecy, like this from *Young Mistley,* to which time has given authority: "One day Central Asia will be opened out, suddenly and completely, by the biggest fight the world has ever seen. It has not come in my time, it may not come in Mistley's; but come it will, as sure as fate" (59).[9]

The narrative thread of the story is thus frequently interrupted for confidences to the reader. Such confidences were usually to foreshadow action or to deliver an aphoristic generalization. Sometimes the foreshadowing tends to synopsize future action, as ". . . at the moment he did not attach much importance to the suspicion, though he remembered it later," or "He saw how the land lay, and knew that his reward would be greater than his deserts" (88–9). A rather extended aphorism is illustrated by the following typical aside: "You and I, fellow-traveller, can smile a little too. We know what a fell destroyer of man's career that tiny-winged god can be, when once he gets his range and settles to his aim. We know that ambition crumbles away before love, as a sandheap before the rising tide" (73).

That there was the same apparent conflict being waged in the author's mind between love and glory, and that love was to win— as it did in fact win less than a year later—is affirmed by his writing, "could it be that there are, after all, other things in life worth striving for than fame, and the glory of placing one's chiselled stone in the great structure of an empire?" (73).

The author's descriptive passages were generally graphic, although his language sometimes became labored: "The moon had bravely taken up her mighty task of sweeping clear the heavens. But there were some huge clouds that promised to strain her cleansing powers to the utmost . . . the moon had set to work with all the ardor of a new broom. Here and there in the clouded vault little puffs of silvery white betrayed weak spots in the canopy of vapor; and through these the white scavenger was boring assiduously, leaving no breach unattempted" (143).

II   The Phantom Future

The next three novels in this early group of four rejected by the author were published quickly, as were most of the author's books. *The Phantom Future,* in fact, appeared in the same year as *Young Mistley. Phantom,* even more than *Mistley,* stresses the importance of establishing a plan or purpose in life and of adhering vigorously to it. The book also contains the first of Merriman's gallery of studies in the deterioration of character. A third thematic element involves an indictment of England's class system, the practices of which, as in the situation described in the story, often result in tragedy.

The Phantom Future is a sort of *Vie de Bohème* on a highly moral tone transported to the London scene. It is one of the few novels written by Merriman that, departing from his usual pattern of transferring action back and forth between the domestic and the foreign locale, confine their action to England. The subject matter may substantiate the assertion that the author was somewhat influenced by a study of French literary models.

The story is concerned with the fortunes and misfortunes of a group of medical students, artists, and writers who are accustomed to frequent a restaurant-bar presided over by a superior young woman of the lower class whom the students call Syra. The use of such a place as a unifying device for the activities of so diverse a group of characters sometimes creates confusion in continuity. The Bohemian temperament, furthermore, is one with which the author has little sympathy and less patience. Sympathy is created for the doomed artist-medico Tom Valliant, but it is obtained through contemptuous pity rather than through true appreciation for the nuances in Tom's character. With the strong and purposeful journalist and singer, Samuel Crozier, the author is on surer ground. Crozier represents the qualities of durability and individualism that Merriman most admired; admired, indeed, to the point of close identification with the character. On occasion Crozier becomes his creator's mouthpiece, as in this passage where Merriman virtually summarized his own biography:

Concealment leaves its mark upon man. I know a man who is now a celebrated writer [who but Merriman himself!], but his own name is quite unknown. When he was young he lived a double life. In his family he was merely the second son—a Government clerk, with no great prospect of advancement. Under his assumed name he was one of the most prominent literary men of his day. Of course it was a mistake; but he began with the idea of suppressing his identity with the promising writer until he was sure of his success, and then it was difficult to tell the secret (101).[10]

Of Crozier as hero—as a man with a plan in life who steadfastly follows his own star—the author writes: "In short, the man was strong, with that great, deep, enduring strength which is independent of human sympathies. Few men of this stamp pass through their allotted years without doing some good, lightening some burdens, and holding up some stumblers. . . . the lives around them if not brighter, are surer in their brightness and braver in their shadows for the unconscious influence wielded by strength over great and small" (74). True to the author's heroic pattern, however, Crozier, for all his strength, was not lacking in the essential quality of gentility; for "In all circles and under all circumstances he had experienced no difficulty in steering his own course, guided by that subtle sense of refinement which is the true instinct of gentlemanliness" (83).

In this book, as in most of his others, the author's attempts at the light touch are generally either out of character or labored. On one occasion, the barmaid, Syra, remarks to a patron, "You have grown very abstemious" (184). Tom says ponderously, "Then do not open them [letters] that these ears may be spared the shock of an expletive" (26). Crozier's playfulness is equally heavy in "The pot is casting aspersions upon the complexion of the kettle" (52). That the author himself may have been conscious of a certain lack of inventiveness is apparent from one of his numerous asides to the effect that "there is a sad want of economy in everyday life. It is like a very large book with a small plot and few incidents. We take a long time to do very little; in fact, to use a technical expression, there is too much padding" (181).

Criticism of this book, like that of *Mistley,* was sparse and perfunctory. Merriman had not yet established himself as a real contender in the bid for popularity.

III   Suspense

Merriman's third novel, *Suspense,* illustrates varying degrees of narrative skill. After his exclusive preoccupation with the domestic scene in *Phantom Future,* the author returns to the imperialistic pattern: the action of this book opens out from England to the European continent, especially Bulgaria and the other countries involved in the Russo-Turkish war. This experiment in interweaving history with fiction was one which Merriman repeated effectively in many later novels. Such a combination, in fact, provided him with the necessary broad canvas for the type of swashbuckling adventure which he seemed to be most effective in depicting. This story, in particular, rises to its greatest height of interest and eloquence when the author relates the story of the siege of Plevna. The historical facts behind Skobeleff's capture of the Bulgarian town, the bloody battle itself, and the eventual dislodgment of the Russians by the Turks under the wily Osman Pasha are presented dramatically and forcefully.

Moreover, at least one of the fictional characters in the story achieves a genuine, if transient reality, despite the aura of melodrama and the too evident maneuvering of fate in the background. This character is the war correspondent and adventurer Theodore Trist, whose creation may have been suggested to

Merriman by the exploits of his father's friend, Frederic Villiers. Trist is a self-sufficient and uncommunicative hero who sacrifices love and his own life to duty. Moreover, the circumstances that dictate his activities are very credible, and Trist himself is fully realized as a person.

Interesting as the tale is, there are many digressive elements and subplots that make it difficult to focus the attention on the main stream of action. Coincidence is perhaps overemphasized in the disposal of characters and in the resolution of situations; and the author's admiration for the British Empire, as well as his predilection for the hackneyed phrase in conjunction with his sometimes sententious philosophizing, is frequently on view.

The plot is designed to document the theme of the book: the superiority of the individual who doggedly and selflessly performs his duty as he sees it. Theodore Trist, the war correspondent, exemplifies this theme. He and Brenda Gilholme, the niece of Admiral Wylie, are in love, but neither declares that love: he, because he feels that no one engaged in his dangerous occupation has a right to ask a woman to share that danger; she, because she fears that Trist may still be in love, as he in fact once was, with her sister Alice, who is now unhappily married to the wastrel Alfred Huston. Trist recovers the body of Admiral Wylie from a Norwegian fjord after the Admiral is accidentally drowned from his yacht. After the Wylies' return to England, Trist also tries unsuccessfully to right the marital difficulties of Alice and her husband.

If the characters, aside from Trist, seem somewhat shallow, this lack of depth must be attributed to the code under which they lived. Brenda Gilholme epitomizes this attitude of passive acceptance. The author says of her:

In a vague, indefinite way she was realizing that woman is weaker than man—is, in fact, a weaker man, with smaller capabilities of joy and sorrow, of love, hatred, devotion, or remorse; and, in a way William Hicks profited by this thought. She respected him—not individually, but generally—because he was a man; and because she felt that some women could look up to him and admire him for his mere manhood (107–8).[11]

Merriman's aphorisms, in this as in his other books, occur frequently. In this respect, however, he was doing no more than reflecting the taste of his era. Many of them are truisms, but relevant ones with a universal application. "There are people," he says on one occasion, "who while seeking to render themselves valuable to the many, are of use to none" (56). Other similar statements seem to have ironic overtones, as when he says wryly, "War is the path by which the world progresses" (212). Merriman sometimes satirized the English caste system, but he nevertheless makes his position clear respecting the code of the gentleman. "Despite his dissipated air," he says of Alfred Huston, "there was that indefinite sense of refinement which belongs to birth and breeding, and which never leaves a man who has once moved among gentlemen" (108).

IV Prisoners and Captives

While *Prisoners and Captives,* the fourth of this early group of novels, does not completely solve the problem of unity of action, it is a vast improvement in this respect over *Suspense.* In *Prisoners* Merriman returns to the Nihilistic theme. Specifically, the story is designed to emphasize the terrible sacrifices that must be made in the continuing war of freedom against the forces of tyranny, and to do so by showing the impact of tragedy on several lives as a result of the Nihilist revolt against the Russian Czar. There are several scenes in which the realistic details are brutal enough to satisfy the confirmed Naturalist. The rescue of Claude Tyars from the fever-stricken ship *Martial;* Tyars's heroic action in saving the lives of Oswin and Helen Grace, Mark Easton, and Agnes Winter in the theater fire; and the terrible death of the Russian political prisoners on the Siberian steppes as a result of the abortive and quixotic rescue scheme devised by Tyars and Easton—these are among the most impressive scenes of this type.

There are many similarities in the plot situations of *Suspense* and *Prisoners and Captives,* but the latter is much the better book. *Prisoners* shows growth in several respects: the characters are more fully developed and more sharply differentiated; the plot elements, while still somewhat diverse, are nevertheless powerful and show a greater tendency toward cohesiveness; and the author's probing of the social conscience of his time is more skillful and more thorough.

This last improvement is due, in large part, to the introduction of the American, Matthew Mark Easton. Be it recorded to Merriman's credit, moreover, that this American is neither the fool nor the scoundrel whom British novelists of the period were fond of flaying in their works. Instead, Easton is a competent, intelligent observer of the British scene and makes a perfect mouthpiece for the author's satirical or cynical comments about social mores. "Very few of us," says Easton, "do trouble our heads about social problems. We leave them to those acrimonious and long-winded gentlemen who write for the reviews" (120).[12] On another occasion he continues, "Then in England, as well as in my own country, charity is a recognized plaything of society" (128). So interested was Merriman in this thesis that he was to incorporate it as one of the themes in *Roden's Corner.*

Concerning the British class system, Easton (and incidentally the author) is more eloquent. He respects "your British institutions and your domestic servants; the two hold together right through. Half the institutions are adhered to on account of the servants. Half your British gentlemen dress for dinner because their butler puts on a clawhammer coat for the same. Half your ladies wash their hands for lunch because the hired girl has taken up a tin of hot water" (91).

In his own person, the author speaks even more forcefully concerning the frustrations and the economic inequities of the world around him. "Suspicion fixes herself upon the impecunious, the unfortunate, the low in station. She haunts the area-steps and flies at the luxurious sound of carriage-wheels. . . . Well dressed we may steal horses, shabbily clad we must not even look over walls" (91). And "The truth of the matter is, that ladies and gentlemen of this latter end of the nineteenth century are difficult subjects to write about. They will not, like folks upon the stage, make facial contortions capable of record as showing inward emotions. . . . They are so persistently self-possessed that one cannot wring a dramatic situation out of them anyhow" (194–95). This last observation may have been offered as an explanation to critics who accused Merriman of refusing to portray strong emotion.

These four novels, though rejected by their creator, show some interesting sidelights on the development of a writer. From *Young Mistley* to *Prisoners and Captives* there is a definite progression from a loose to a concise, economical narration. The characters too show an increasing tendency to round out into completely differentiated individuals. Theodore Trist, for instance, is a more fully realized human being than Winyard Mistley. Although they are emancipated thus in space, they are circumscribed in time; they continue to be bound, as indeed they should, by the conventions of their era. The author's skill as a teller of tales, apparent in *Mistley,* is confirmed in *Prisoners;* and his themes are diverse enough to reveal the many-faceted aspects of the social group which he portrayed. His tendency toward extensive use of the epigram is also a reflection of the taste of his time, and *Prisoners* shows that he is learning to control this propensity for generalization within more specific boundaries. The author's decision to avoid realistic techniques apparently extends only to the limits of his homeland. He never descends to "flaunting the seamy side," yet he exhibits considerable skill in the use of realistic detail in description of the foreign scene.

CHAPTER 3

The Major Novels

FROM the time of publication of Merriman's next novel until his death, he wrote a total of seventeen books. By no means could all of these be considered major works. Among them were a book of character sketches, a volume of essays, and a collection of short stories. These will be dealt with in another chapter. One of the novels, *Dross,* the author withdrew from publication. Seven or eight of the remaining thirteen deserve a high place among romantic adventure stories.

The publication of *The Slave of the Lamp* in 1892 marked a milestone in Merriman's career. In fact, it might almost be regarded as his personal declaration of independence, for it was in 1892 that he decided to forsake business permanently in favor of letters. He was not, however, ready at this time to reveal to his family the true identity of Henry Seton Merriman. Perhaps he felt that his success as a writer was not yet firmly enough established to convince his father of the wisdom of his decision.

I The Slave of the Lamp

Having had some success with a journalistic hero in *Suspense,* Merriman chose another such in *The Slave of the Lamp,* a much more unified story than its predecessor. In fact, except for an attack upon the Jesuits and a reliance upon fate to resolve some of the difficulties of the plot, this book is a well-balanced example of the tale of romantic intrigue that contains enough historical detail to convey credibility.

The story is concerned with the activities of Christian Vellacott, star reporter of the *Beacon,* who lives in lodgings in the London of the 1890's, where he cares for two querulous and mentally unbalanced old aunts, Judy and Hester. His employers, Bodery and Martin, insist that he take a vacation; and after engaging a nurse to care for the old aunts during his absence, he visits his old friends the Carews at their country home.

Meanwhile, the Vicomte d'Audierne, Father Max Talma, and the laborer Lerac have been plotting a revolt against the French Republic in the back room of Jacquetot's tobacco shop in Paris. D'Audierne is known there simply as Citizen Morot. The conspirators have been receiving guns and ammunition from England. These they store, in preparation for the projected uprising, in a monastery. They fear that Vellacott may get wind of their plans, and Talma is dispatched to spy on him while he is on vacation.

Arrived at the Carews', Vellacott renews his acquaintance with the beautiful Hilda Carew, whom he had known as a child. Without revealing their feelings to each other, they believe themselves in love, though Hilda is engaged to Fred Farrar, Squire of St. Mary Eastern. Vellacott meets a friend of the Carews, Signor Bruno, who seems to him familiar. Scarcely arrived, he receives a letter from Bodery which speaks of the incipient revolt in France and advises that Christian may have to go there should trouble break out. Vellacott prophesies that he can identify Bruno, who, he tells Hilda, is not really the kind old man he seems to be. He accomplishes this feat by telegraphing for information to a friend who had known Talma. He deduces Bruno's connection with the French revolt and the fact that arms and ammunition are being stored nearby in a ruined monastery for shipment to France.

The Jesuit Abbé Drucquer, assigned by the Jesuits to kidnap Vellacott, succeeds by making it appear that the reporter has been drowned in the moat of the old monastery. Vellacott is taken aboard a fishing boat. A storm comes up, nearly wrecking the boat and killing the fisherman in charge. Drucquer is greatly upset by the turn of events and filled with admiration for the heroism of Vellacott, who saves them all in spite of the fact that he is obviously very ill. Vellacott is taken to Brittany and virtually imprisoned in a monastery by the Provincial of the Jesuit order. He is placed under the care of an old priest who has medical knowledge and who nurses him through his fever. Drucquer, influenced by Vellacott, is sent as a missionary to avoid the more active intrigues of the Jesuits.

More than three months go by, and the Carews fear that Vellacott is really drowned. Hilda is greatly saddened, but she remains silent about their regard for each other. The Provincial who holds Vellacott is a dedicated zealot determined to protect the Jesuits against further newspaper attacks by Vellacott, who had published an article before his capture revealing the whole French plot and the Jesuits' part in it.

After recovering from his fever, Vellacott manages to escape from the monastery and to board a brig on the Channel coast. Crossing the Channel, his boat passes another ship and Vellacott recognizes Talma aboard. Talma sees him also and tries to shoot him to prevent a successful escape, but Talma drops dead with a stroke of apoplexy. When he arrives at his home in London, Vellacott finds that Aunt Judy has died and that Mrs. Carew and Hilda have been called in to care for Aunt Hester. He is about to declare his love to Hilda when she informs him that she has married Fred in the interim, realizing that it was really Fred that she loved and believing Vellacott to be dead. It is then revealed, too late, that Christian had given a letter to Drucquer to be delivered to the Carews at the time of his capture, but Drucquer had burned the letter.

The uprising has broken out in Paris, and the Vicomte is seriously wounded fighting at the barricades before the revolt is put down. Mysteriously, the Provincial rescues him and brings him to Jacquetot's shop in Paris. There it is revealed that the Vicomte and the Provincial are actually brothers.

Years later, Vellacott, a very successful and respected journalist, meets Drucquer aboard a ship returning from India. Drucquer is fatally stricken with fever and he tells Vellacott that he had burnt the letter he was to deliver to the Carews. Thus, as so often in Hardy's novels, lives are altered by the nondelivery of a letter.

Again, this book stresses the necessity for sacrificing personal desires to duty, but the author seems to be particularly concerned with exploring the role of fate in altering human destiny. Chance or fate makes it possible for Christian Vellacott, the reporter hero, to deduce in advance the nature of the aristocratic-Jesuit plot against the French Republic. Thus Vellacott becomes a sort of superintellect whose powers are not explained. Vellacott again owes his life to the intervention of fate when the arch-plotter, Father Max Talma, fortuitously drops dead in the act of firing a pistol at him at point-blank range. Finally, Father Drucquer's destruction of the letter Vellacott wrote to his friends, the Carews, after he had been kidnaped by the Jesuits, makes it possible for Hilda Carew to misinterpret Vellacott's silence, thus permitting the novel to end on a typical note of blighted romance, rounded out with a "years later" anticlimax in which Vellacott is revealed as a highly successful journalist, but also as a lonely, loveless man.

The author's strong feeling against Roman Catholicism and the Jesuits is apparent throughout the book, but it is especially notice-able in the following passages:

A true Jesuit must have no nature of his own and no individuality. He is simply a machine, with likes and dislikes, conscience and soul subject to the will of the next in authority, whose mind is also under the arbi-trary control of his superior; and so on to the top. If at the head there were God, it would be well; but man is there, and consequently the whole society is a gigantic mistake. To be a sincere member of it, a man must be a half-witted fool, a religious fanatic, or a rogue for whom no duplicity is too scurrilous, even though it amount to blas-phemy (209–10).[1]

. . . .

The creed they [the Jesuits] taught without understanding it them-selves was that no man must give way to natural impulses; that he must restrain and quell and quench himself into a machine, without individuality or impulse, without likes or dislikes; that he must persist-ently perform such duties as are abhorrent to him, eat such food as nauseates him, and submit to the dictates of such men as hate him. And these, forsooth, are the teachings of one who, in his zealous short-sightedness, claims to have received his inspiration direct from the lips of the Great Teacher (217).

It seems possible that Father Talma and his superior, the Pro-vincial, are modeled after Thackeray's great Jesuit, Father Holt. This possibility is supported by their multitudinous intrigues and disguises and by their common concern with Royalist plots against republicanism. Merriman identifies Thackeray as "the king of writers" (150). Thus we can be sure that he was familiar with the exploits of Father Holt. But whereas Father Holt, despite his plots and counterplots, was essentially a sympathetic character, the Provincial to a large extent, and Father Talma absolutely, ex-hibit few traits that might recommend them to our esteem. Father Holt was motivated by devotion to a cause; Father Talma seems to respond primarily to the stimulus of self-aggrandizement and power.

The influences of other novelists are apparent in *The Slave of the Lamp*. The gentle insanities of Vellacott's Aunts Judith and Hester and the Pickwickian natures of Messrs. Bodery and Martin, Vellacott's employers, would probably not have been possible had not Dickens preceded Merriman. The overdependence on fate, apparent in many of Merriman's books no less than in this one, might find its precedent in a similar tendency exhibited in the novels of Thomas Hardy.

As in many of his other stories, Merriman is particularly happy in this one in his description of places. The opening chapters of the book, which sketch in the environment for intrigue through a detailed and vivid description of M. Jacquetot and his shop in the Rue Gingolphe, are especially evocative in this respect. The events centering around Jacquetot and his shop where the conspirators met, in conjunction with the frequent shifting of scene from London to Paris, are surely not merely accidental parallels to the events occurring at the Defarges' and a similar shift of scene in Dickens' *A Tale of Two Cities*.

The *Athenaeum* review judges as absurd the plot conceit that a British citizen could be kidnaped with impunity by the Jesuits.[2] However, this imaginative hurdle, "suggestive of the rack and the Inquisition," is one which the reader must take without balking if he is to enjoy the excitement and intrigue of the story as a whole. What is required of the reader is akin to the "willing suspension of disbelief" called for by Coleridge. From the internal evidence concerning Jesuit activities, there is, implicitly, more than a hint that the author shaped the plot of this book to suit his thesis.

II   From One Generation to Another

From One Generation to Another, also published in 1892, explores as its principal theme the corroding effect on human personality of a long-nourished desire for revenge. In this respect, the book is essentially a psychological study of character deterioration and self-destruction under the impetus of a perverse emotional drive. A secondary but apparent thematic development is the author's antagonistic attitude toward a representative of the Jewish race. The villain of *From One Generation to Another* happens to be a Jew, and a considerable racial antagonism is cumulated upon this figure.

The character in question is Seymour Michael, a man of intrigue and an officer in the colonial army in India during and after the Mutiny. Michael decides that he would rather marry the daughter of a wealthy colonial than the girl to whom he is betrothed, Anna Hethbridge, the middle-class daughter of a well-to-do Clapham merchant. When his death is mistakenly reported, he remains silent, allowing Anna to think he has really been killed; but he does not get to marry the wealthy colonial after all.

Six months later, Anna, while visiting the family of the Reverend Thomas Glynde, the comfort-loving and worldly rector of Stagholme in Hertfordshire, marries the middle-aged James Edward Agar, a widower and the Squire of Stagholme. He has a young son, James, upon whom Anna mistakenly tries to force herself. When she is about to bear a child to the Squire, she learns from a returned Indian soldier that Michael is not dead; that he has, in fact, boasted about the trick he used to get out of an engagement. Since he is a shrewd opportunist, he is rising rapidly in the Indian service.

While Michael is home on leave, Anna invites him to visit her and she confronts him with her knowledge, swearing to get even someday and calling him a "mean, lying Jew." This so infuriates Michael that he too determines to be revenged on her. Arthur, Anna's son, is born prematurely that night.

When James passes the age of twenty-one, Anna, his stepmother who has never liked him, schemes to get him a commission in an Indian Goorkha regiment, a very dangerous post where she hopes he may be killed so that her weakling and petted son, Arthur, may inherit Stagholme. Dora Glynde, the rector's daughter, has been attracted to James, but he is too full of plans for becoming a soldier to be interested in romance. James goes to India and is soon sent on a suicidal mission to hold a mountain position with a small band of Indian soldiers until relief arrives. It does not arrive in time, and James is reported dead.

Eventually Michael, now a general, arrives to relieve James; and he plans, since James is already reported dead, to send him in disguise on a dangerous mission to spy out the territory between India and Russia and to try to find out Russia's intentions in re-

gard to India. James accedes; but he makes Michael promise that
he will tell the truth to Anna, Arthur, and Dora Glynde. This Michael promises to do, since he is soon to retire to England after
thirty years in the Indian service.

Meanwhile, though he is a poor student, Arthur has been sent
to Cambridge. Anna, believing James to be dead, has been con-
sulting lawyers about Arthur's inheriting the estate, and she urges
marriage between Arthur and Dora Glynde. This union is agreeable to Dora's parents but not to Dora, who still loves James but
manages to conceal her grief for him.

Michael comes back to England and reveals the truth about
James to Arthur, but he swears Arthur to secrecy, hoping thus to
torture Anna by making her believe more firmly that Stagholme
is really her son's. Besides, Michael says that the mission is so
dangerous that James is as good as dead. He knows, furthermore,
that, if the mission is not successful, it will be more to his personal
credit as a general if the facts are never revealed.

Thus the situation remains for several months until James, successful in his mission, takes ship for home. Aboard ship he learns
of the villainy of Michael from the ship's doctor, Mark Ruthine,
who is acquainted with the whole story. Arrived home, accompanied by Ruthine, James seeks out Michael and forces him to go
to Stagholme to reveal the facts. Arthur has already noticed that
he feels a strange repulsion toward Michael; and, even before he
learns of the injury that Michael had formerly done to his mother,
as well as the truth about James, he goes berserk, pursues Michael
out of the house, and kills him. Arthur's action is explained on the
basis that he was "marked" at birth by his mother's unreasoning
hatred of Michael, having been born on the night that Anna had
sworn vengeance against Michael. Thus Anna's revenge is brought
about and so is Michael's on Anna, for Arthur is in a cataleptic
coma and may not recover. James and Dora are united at last.

Although the consequences of Anna's scheme to get even with
Michael are highly melodramatic, this story of revenge which is
passed down from mother to son, to the ultimate ruin of one and
the death of the other, is tightly plotted; and it moves to its in-
exorable conclusion much like a Greek tragedy. In fact, it is this
resemblance to drama—this quality of staginess—that makes the
scenes in the novel seem contrived for effect.

As is true of most of Merriman's novels, the descriptions of places in India as well as in England are generally excellent. The social commentary in the book is skillfully handled as an adjunct to character delineation. Thus it is said satirically of Squire Agar that "The bourgeois ostentation and would-be high toned graciousness of the ladies jarred on his nerves as harshly as did the personal appearance of their respective husbands" (13).[3] Again, "The bourgeois mind, with its love of a Crystal Palace, a subscription dance, or even a parochial bazaar, was unquenchable even after years of practice as the county lady of supremacy" (101).

The author, however, is quite seriously defining his conception of the Englishman as a hero when he says: "Such it is to be an Englishman—the product of an English public school and country life. Thick-limbed, very quiet; thick-headed if you will!—that is as may be—but with a nerve of iron, ready to face the last foe of all—death, without so much as a wink" (67).

He returns to the attack on society with "Why, oh, why, does bereavement drive women into bath-chairs on the King's road, or the Lee or the Hoe? With many the display of sympathy is nothing but a half-conscious bait to attract a shoal of further details" (121). On another occasion he observes "Society is not allowed to stand for cream now. It is stirred up with a spoon, silver-gilt, and the skim milk gets hopelessly mixed up with the cream" (154).

The destructive psychological effects of a desire for vengeance are presented effectively through the deterioration of the characters of the people involved. Furthermore, Merriman's concentration upon race as the clue to character—a philosophy he applies rigorously to the Anglo-Saxon—he turns also upon a principal of the Jewish race.

He [Michael] was dark of hair, with a sallow complexion and a long, drooping nose—the nose of Semitic ancestors   (2).

. . . .

He knew that he only possesseed one thing to risk, namely, his life; and true to his racial instinct he valued this very highly, looking for an extortionate usury on his stake   (3).

. . . .

Here again was the taint of blood that ran in his veins. The curse had reached to him—in addition to the long, sad nose and the bandy legs   (5).

. . . .

A joke of this description made him feel rather sick, for a Jew never makes a soldier or a sailor, and they are rarely found in those positions unless great gain is holden up (7).

. . . .

It is very difficult to bring shame home to a Jew, and on that occasion this son of the modern Ishmaelite had been thoroughly ashamed of himself (129).

Although Merriman was by no means alone in the practice of using foreign speech tags in the nineteenth century, he had a fondness for sprinkling his manuscript with French phrases or with linguistic archaisms to lend tone and effect. Occasionally such old-fashioned words point up the charm or satire of the story, but such expressions as "holden" for "held," "hight" for "named," and "wot" for "knew" are simply excrescences.

The literary journals were almost unanimous in praising the story-telling ability exhibited in *From One Generation to Another,* but they attacked the author for doing that which they had formerly blamed him for not doing—analyzing character realistically and in depth. The reviewers also agreed on the improbable aspects of many situations in the story. Among these are the manner in which Michael is able to conceal from everyone that he had not really died during the Indian Mutiny but yet was able to retain his military connection, and the providential means by which the ship's doctor, Mark Ruthine, had gained prior knowledge of Anna's complicated scheme to permit her worthless son, Arthur, to inherit Stagholme. The reader is faced with similar loose ends when the author disposes of the wealthy colonial girl whom Michael was originally supposed to marry by simply allowing her to disappear from view. Furthermore, no preparation or natural explanation is given for Arthur's final violence and madness.

The London *Bookman* compares *From One Generation to Another* to *Slave of the Lamp,* calling each equally able and equally improbable. Both the *Bookman* and the *Athenaeum* note the author's apparent animosity toward certain racial or religious groups —particularly toward the Jews as represented by Michael, and toward the Church of England as represented by the grasping Reverend Glynde and the hypocritical Sister Cecelia[4] but they omit mentioning the fact that such an unattractive female as

Cecelia is balanced by the virtuous and womanly Dora Glynde. The *Athenaeum* labels the book "thoroughly misanthropic . . . full of Jew-baiting and animosity toward the middle class and the church." [5] The author, the review continues, proves his ability to write a "disagreeable story without recourse to naturalistic methods." [6]

Paradoxically, some of the reviewer's objections stem from the fact that Merriman, consciously or not, actually did apply the Naturalistic technique to the characters in attempting to explore the psychological motives which prompted their reprehensible acts. None of them is wholly bad. Michael is driven by an instinct he cannot control; Anna has strong provocation and her later actions are governed by a natural but unbalanced maternalism; Sister Cecelia, however hypocritical, does have a strong but misdirected sense of loyalty to her friend Anna; even the Reverend Glynde's ambition for a union between his daughter and Arthur is based partially on his desire to see Dora well established in life.

III With Edged Tools

Before his next novel was published in 1894, Merriman collaborated with his sister-in-law on a volume of essays that will be discussed in the chapter about his miscellaneous work. The year 1894 also marked the publication of one of the seven or eight best books of his entire career and the best of all his stories up to this time—*With Edged Tools*. This book also first established him in the front rank of popularity among the romancers of his day.[7] More effectively than any of his preceding works, this book illustrates Merriman's ability to blend romance with the realism of the analytical novel. In fact, so realistic was the story that readers wrote to the publishers asking if they could buy shares in the Simiacine Company formed by the leading characters, Guy Oscard, Jack Meredith, and Victor Durnovo. "The character of the slave-trafficking, ruthless Durnovo, the journey up-river, and the camp at Msala [in Africa] are worthy of Conrad, and Haggard might envy Durnovo's nightmarish mutilation and horrible death in gibbering terror of the sleeping sickness." [8]

In respect to theme, *With Edged Tools* is somewhat akin to Butler's *Way of All Flesh*. Both examine the concept of the authoritarian family and the result of defiance of this authority, especially in the case of Jack Meredith and Millicent Chyne. The book also celebrates the spirit of empire and of the sturdy individuals, like Meredith and Oscard, who braved the dangers and terrors of savage lands to mold that empire. In this, as in his books with Indian backgrounds, there is evidence of similarities to the work of Kipling. The author's interest in applying psychological principles to the interpretation of character is apparent not only in the masterly study of the scoundrelly Durnovo, but in the objectively drawn portrait of the coquette, Millicent Chyne, who overreaches herself in a greedy desire to make doubly sure of an advantageous marriage.

The story deals with the activities of a number of people in the forefront of London society and with their interrelationships with some natives and white traders in West Africa. Jack Meredith chafes under the authority of his autocratic father, Sir John Meredith, who has warned his son against marrying the flirtatious, empty-headed Millicent Chyne, the niece and ward of his lifelong friend, Lady Caroline Cantourne. Sir John and Lady Cantourne have lived a life of mutual regret for having allowed social conventions to dissuade them from marrying in their youth. As a result of his father's disapproval, Jack breaks with Sir John and decides to seek his fortune in West Africa, completely independent of his family. Accordingly, he obtains Millicent's promise to wait for him and goes to Africa to join partnership with Victor Durnovo, a half-caste trader in goods and slaves, in the cultivation and marketing of Simiacine, a drug of marvelous curative powers derived from a plant that grows wild in the interior of Africa. In Africa Jack meets the white trader, Maurice Gordon, who seeks to conceal his past activity in slave traffic, and his gentle and understanding sister, Jocelyn, who falls in love with Jack.

Guy Oscard is the big-game hunting son of the scholar and historian, Thomas Oscard, whose fear of insanity drives him to frequent attempts at suicide. One such attempt is successful; and, since Guy is in the house at the time, many of his acquaintances blame him for not having taken proper precautions to prevent his father's death. To escape these unjust accusations, he too goes to Africa where he subsequently joins Jack and Durnovo in the Simiacine partnership. Before his departure, Millicent tentatively pledges herself to him because Oscard has already inherited a comfortable income and she fears that Jack may not be successful in establishing his own fortune.

In Africa, an expedition is formed to visit and inspect the Simiacine plantation. On the way, the camp is stricken with smallpox at Msala. On the pretense of seeking medicine, Durnovo deserts the expedition and returns to the settlement at Loango. The smallpox is conquered, Guy brings Durnovo back by force, and they eventually locate the Simiacine. Guy and Durnovo come back with a shipment of Simiacine, which Guy takes to England to sell. Again Durnovo deserts, leaving Jack on the plateau surrounded by unfriendly native tribes. Durnovo is supposed to bring back assistance, but instead he pays court to Jocelyn, who despises him. He threatens to expose her brother's slave-trading activities unless she marries him. This she refuses to do.

Several months later when Jocelyn has learned from a letter brought down from the camp that Jack is desperately ill, she telegraphs Guy to return to the rescue. All this time, both Jack and Guy have been corresponding with Millicent, each assuming that he is to marry her and each unaware of the fact that both love the same girl.

Guy comes to the rescue; Jack is brought down to Msala by his manservant, Joseph; and Durnovo and Guy quarrel. Guy has learned that Durnovo's natives on the expedition are really his slaves, and he offers to take them back and release them. Unaccountably, they elect to remain on the plateau with Durnovo, who expects to reap the remaining benefit from the Simiacine, since Guy has dissolved the partnership.

Maurice and Jocelyn go to England on vacation. There Sir John meets Jocelyn and determines that she is the woman Jack should marry. When they return to Loango, Jocelyn finds Jack recuperating under the care of Joseph. She nurses him back to health and he is ordered to return to England by the doctor. Joseph and Guy remain behind to settle the Simiacine affair.

One night Durnovo comes to them half mad with fear, with his eyelids, lips, and ears cut off. His men have turned against him, tortured him, and chased him away from the plateau. Later he dies of the sleeping sickness which had broken out in the camp. Thus Gordon's secret is buried with Durnovo. Guy and Joseph realize that this will mean that the whole expedition at the Simi-acine plateau will be wiped out. They determine never to have anything more to do with the scheme, hence the Simiacine venture is lost to mankind.

In London, Jack's plans to wed Millicent go forward in spite of his father's continued opposition. Sir John has surmised Millicent's duplicity; and, when Guy returns to London he takes him to the house where Jack and Millicent, whose wedding is to take place the next day, are looking at some of their wedding presents. When Jack and Guy meet in Millicent's presence, her deceit is revealed. Both men refuse to have anything more to do with her, and she is left presumably to explain her jilting as best she can. Guy goes to India hunting big game; Jack goes to Europe without making up with his father, though he now realizes Sir John was right. Lady Cantourne forgives Sir John for revealing the situation to Guy and Jack, for she realizes that Millicent is an incurable flirt. When Jack returns and makes up the quarrel with his father, Sir John advises him to go to Africa and bring back Jocelyn as his wife. This he does, but his telegraph message telling his father that he and Jocelyn are returning finds Sir John dead in his bed.

With Edged Tools is definitely superior to Merriman's earlier work. Theme and tone are sustained, and most of the characters grow and develop in the course of the story. Particularly worth appreciation are Sir John Meredith and his son, both of whom voluntarily depart from their original stiff-necked positions. Sir John learns to temper his uncompromising Victorian authoritarianism with forgiveness in a time of rapidly shifting social values, and Jack comes to know the wisdom and value of family solidarity. Even the opportunistic Millicent realizes at last the error of her ways when she is deserted by both of her suitors. While Durnovo's villainy is unredeemed to the end, his portrait is a masterly study in criminal psychology.

Numerous passages in the book document Merriman's authority as spokesman for the social and moral code of his time. Concerning the gulf between the classes—between the gentleman and the man—Jack says, "He knew that this man was not a gentleman, but his own position was so assured that he could afford to asso-

ciate with anyone" (52).[9] Again, "If Joseph had not been my
domestic servant, I should have liked him for a friend" (125), or
"Truly, the modern English gentleman is a strange being . . . .
You cannot educate the manliness out of him, try as you will"
(85).

The author is always careful to clear up any hint of sexual
irregularity, as when the half-caste Marie assures Oscard that the
dead Victor Durnovo had been her husband, not her lover. " 'It
is all right,' said Marie bluntly. " 'We were married at Sierra
Leone by the English Chaplain' " (292).

Concerning woman's place in society, the author says that
"woman is too delicate a social flower to be independent of en-
vironments. She takes the tone of her surroundings" (52), and
hence must be protected. Even the hardy but beautiful Jocelyn,
who has spent a good share of her life in Africa on the frontiers
of the empire, is unable to say certain things because "all the
advanced females in the world, all the blue stockings and divided
skirts, all the wild women and those who pant for burdens other
than children will never bring it to pass that women can say such
things" (157). This passage makes it clear, however, that some of
the emancipated bluestockings so thoroughly disliked by Merriman were beginning to say "such things," else the author would
not have felt it necessary to inveigh so heavily against their doing
so.

This book, like many of his others, also illustrates the author's
championship of the British Empire ideal. In addition to reflecting a love of travel and adventure, Merriman's frequent and effective use of the foreign scene gives ample opportunity to exploit this theme, as did Kipling's use of the Indian background.
Merriman's attitude toward the borders of empire and the heroes
who pushed those borders before them, and his regret that such
an era is passing, are summed up in the following stirring passage.

There are some Englishmen left, thank Heaven! who love fighting
for its own sake, and not only for the gain of it. Such men as this lived
in the old days of chivalry, at which modern puny carpet-knights make
bold to laugh, while inwardly thanking their stars that they live in the
peaceful age of the policeman. Such men as this ran their thick, simple
heads against many a windmill, couched lance over many a far-fetched

insult, and swung a sword in honour of many a worthless maid; but they made England, my masters. Let us remember that they made England. (55)

Along with Merriman's yearning after a heroic era that was rapidly passing away, he did not hesitate to attack, on the one hand, the materialism of his own age and, on the other, the peculiar snobbery which permitted the upper classes to look upon the laboring man and his work with contempt. He says angrily on one occasion, "but you must remember that we live in an age when money sanctifies everything. Your hands can't get dirty if there is money inside them" (239). His satire of the upper-class attitude toward those not so fortunate is evidenced in this commentary by Sir John Meredith, which is as subtly witty as anything in Oscar Wilde: "I did not know that he was endeavoring to work. I only trust it is not manual labor—it is so injurious to the fingernails. I have no sympathy with a gentleman who imagines that manual labor is compatible with his position, provided that he does not put his hand to the plough in England. . . . If Jack undertakes any work of that description I trust that he will recognize the fact that he forfeits his position by doing so" (116).

Although there is little differentiation in the speech of the various characters and although the speeches themselves are sometimes pompous, the descriptive passages are effective and strongly appealing: "Loango is the reverse of cheerful. To begin with, it is usually raining there. The roar of the surf—than which there are few sadder sounds on earth—fills the atmosphere with a never-ceasing melancholy. The country is over-wooded; the tropical vegetation, the huge tangled African trees, stand almost in the surf; and inland the red serrated hills mount guard in gloomy array" (66).

Many of Merriman's novels make use of foreshadowing as a means of building suspense. There are many examples of this technique in *With Edged Tools*, but this passage virtually synopsizes the whole story: "Neither of them [Jack Meredith and Guy Oscard] suspected that the friendship thus strangely inaugurated at the rifle's mouth was to run through a longer period than the few months required to reach the plateau—that it was, in fact, to extend through that long expedition over a strange country that we call Life, and that it was to stand the greatest test that friendship has to meet with here on earth" (86). Other passages, basically philosophical, occasionally labor a somewhat obvious point: "There is nothing new under the sun—even immediately under it in Central Africa. The only novelty is the human heart— Central Man. That is never stale, and there are depths still unexplored, heights still unattained, warm rivers of love, cold streams of hatred, and vast plains where strange motives grow" (144).

The author's methods of bringing each chapter to a sort of minor climax and of shifting the action frequently from one set of characters to another have the effect of dividing the novel into a succession of scenes like those in a play. This "staginess" and the role of chance or fate in motivating action tend to disturb the illusion of reality. Chance makes it possible for Sir John to discover that Millicent has engaged herself to both Jack and Guy. Fate decrees that Guy shall arrive in England exactly the day before Jack and Millicent are to marry. The outbreak of smallpox in the camp of the adventurers is fortuitous, and fate decrees that Durnovo, as well as the natives he leaves behind, shall die of the sleeping sickness. Thus, by chance, Gordon's secret is safe and the Simiacine is lost forever, since Jack, Guy, and Joseph have sworn never to return to the plateau.

The *Saturday Review* calls *With Edged Tools* the best of Merriman's earlier books, all of which "display a genuine talent for storytelling and are worth reading." [10] The reviewer pays the book a very high compliment when he implies that it is too objective for the big public and too free of sentimentality for the small public. He points out correctly that, while the novel shows excellent craftsmanship, it does not pretend to greatness.

The *Athenaeum* was equally complimentary, as were most of the other reviews. The author is especially praised by the *Athenaeum* for his "crisp and pointed dialogue" and for the "wit and ingenuity" [11] of his moralizing. Most gracious of the reviewers was the one for the *Academy*, who, without analysis, called *With Edged Tools* one of the "most interesting novels of recent years." [12]

IV The Grey Lady

By 1895, when *The Grey Lady* was published, Merriman had arrived at the point when nearly everything he wrote was eagerly sought by publishers. *The Slave of the Lamp* had been serialized in the *Cornhill* in 1892; *With Edged Tools* ran in the *Cornhill* throughout the latter half of 1894 and the first half of 1895;[13] *The Sowers* also appeared in the *Cornhill* in 1895, prior to book publication. According to Merriman's letter[14] to his mother in 1895, in which he revealed his authorship, *The Grey Lady* was then appearing as a serial in the *Windsor Magazine*. This same letter also reveals that he was then on the staff of the *National Observer*, *Black and White*, and *Cornhill* for short stories, and that he was fiction and travel reviewer for the *National Observer*. Many of his short stories, later collected in *Tomaso's Fortune*, were appearing with considerable regularity.

Such popularity, however, would scarcely have been justified on the basis of *The Grey Lady* alone. The chief virtues of this book are some idyllic scenes on the island of Majorca and an intriguing psychological study of a thoroughly disagreeable and vindictive woman. The story explores the corroding effect of greed and passion on several lives. Mrs. Harrington, Mrs. Ingham-Baker, and her daughter, Agatha, love money more than honor. Luke Fitzhenry places human love above honor. The book contrasts the disaster that overtakes these people with the success that crowns the efforts of the scrupulously honorable Henry Fitzhenry and Eve Challoner.

The orphaned twin brothers, Luke and Henry Fitzhenry, return to London after having taken examinations for the navy. Luke, intellectually superior to his brother, has failed while Henry has passed. Since the death of their parents the boys have been cared for by Mrs. Harrington, an old family friend and a presumably wealthy woman living in Grosvenor Square. The sycophantic Mrs. Ingham-Baker lives with Mrs. Harrington as a sort of companion. Mrs. Harrington, furious about Luke's failure, threatens to alter her will. Mrs. Ingham-Baker secretly hopes that she will disinherit both boys in favor of her daughter, Agatha Ingham-Baker, presently away at school. Henry tries to defend his brother; but Luke, embittered, defies Mrs. Harrington and leaves the house.

The scene shifts to an inn in Barcelona where an old sea captain, John Bontnor, unaccountably in the company of Lord Seahampton, is going to bring his niece, Eve Challoner, from Majorca, where her father has just died. Also in Barcelona temporarily is Count de Lhoseta, a wealthy property owner from Majorca who has led a mysterious and lonely life since the death many years before of his wife.

When Henry Fitzhenry's ship, the *Kittiwake,* had earlier put into Majorca, he had been invited to stay at Casa d'Erraha, the estate of Eve's father, Edward Challoner, who was Mrs. Harrington's cousin. There he had, without revealing his feeling, fallen in love with the beautiful Eve. When Edward Challoner died, it was Fitz who sent word to Eve's uncle, Captain Bontnor. In a bit of foreshadowing, Eve hints that she feels there is some mysterious past that linked her father, Mrs. Harrington, and Count Lhoseta.

Although Lhoseta's lawyer tells Eve that her father held the Casa only by a lease which terminated at his death, Count de Lhoseta later apologizes for his action and tells Eve that the terms of the lease were so vague that no one could be sure of them. Therefore, he wishes Eve to accept the Casa. Eve realizes that he is gallantly trying to make her a gift of the Casa, but she nobly refuses it. She goes to live with Captain Bontnor after having also rejected an offer to live with Mrs. Harrington, who believed Eve to be an heiress.

After being turned down by the navy, Luke rises rapidly in the merchant service, becoming a second officer aboard the *Croonah.* When Mrs. Harrington invites Luke to dinner, he renews his acquaintance with Agatha, who, believing that he may be named Mrs. Harrington's heir, flirts outrageously with him. During the evening, a hint of blackmail is apparent in the relationship between Lhoseta and Mrs. Harrington when she demands from him another £500 for household redecorating. Still in pursuit of Luke, Agatha and her mother decide to go to Malta aboard his ship. During this voyage, Luke and Fitz meet again at Gibraltar. Shortly thereafter Luke and Agatha discover that they are really in love, and Luke promises her to become wealthy.

Fitz, Eve, and de Lhoseta meet again at another dinner party at Mrs. Harrington's. There Eve meets a publisher, John Craik, for whom she later writes some Spanish sketches in an effort to assist financially her uncle who has been ruined in a bank failure. At Craik's invitation, Eve goes to London to discuss her work and his offer of a staff position on his magazine. While there she stays with Mrs. Harrington.

In the course of one of the voyages of the *Croonah*, Luke meets Willie Carr, who lives by his wits and who proposes a dishonest scheme to cheat the marine insurance companies. This involves insuring with Lloyd's a ship in a hurricane area twenty-four hours in advance of a predicted hurricane, and then deliberately wrecking the ship. Luke, who has already told Carr that hurricanes are predictable forty-eight hours in advance, is half tempted to this scheme because of his love for Agatha and his desire to make a fortune.

Mrs. Harrington suffers a stroke and has only a short time to live. Fitz is sent for, and to him she reveals that she has in reality only the sum of £50 by way of a fortune. After her death, Fitz reveals his love to Eve, and de Lhoseta mysteriously promises that one day he will reveal to them the secret of his life.

In a last spiteful gesture, Mrs. Harrington had sent a letter to Luke in which she claimed that Fitz was trying to usurp his place in Agatha's affections. Rashly, Luke cables to Carr the signal that a hurricane is expected and plans to wreck the *Croonah* in a storm he knows is approaching. During the actual wrecking of the ship, Luke discovers for the first time that, by some incredible stroke of fate, Agatha and her mother are among the passengers. Luke tells Agatha of his criminal dishonesty for her sake and she is pleased that he should love her more than honor, but she does not tell him that she had come aboard because Mrs. Harrington had previously indicated that she intended making Luke her heir. Agatha is drowned, but Luke and Mrs. Ingham-Baker are rescued. The admiralty court later exonerates Luke, and the truth is never revealed.

Three years later, de Lhoseta visits Fitz and Eve, who have married and settled at Casa d'Erraha. He tells them that long ago Mrs. Harrington had visited him and his wife, Rosa, and that during this visit his wife had been accidentally killed by a fall. Mrs. Harrington had threatened to report that de Lhoseta had killed his wife unless he made regular payments for her support. This arrangement de Lhoseta had agreed to in order to protect his honored name from scandal.

The author manages to invest the character of the gray and bitter Mrs. Harrington with a quality of elemental evil. Her reactions to the various events are psychologically sound and completely consistent with the personality that has been established for her. The ultimate revelation of the hollow nature of her evil masquerade—the vicious blackmail that causes all the trouble—contributes an interesting facet to Mrs. Harrington's character, but it is difficult to understand why the intelligent and innocent de Lhoseta permitted himself to remain in the power of that opportunistic schemer. The serene beauty of the Majorcan Valley of Repose is a pleasant antidote to the evil presentiments of the plot.

Fate plays a prominent role in *The Grey Lady*. The providential manner of the meeting of Eve and Fitz, the chance by which Eve becomes a writer, the accidental meeting of Luke and Carr, and Luke's discovery that Agatha is aboard his ship just at the time he is to wreck it—all these events tend to make the characters mere playthings of fate.

Luke's action in agreeing to wreck his ship in order to collect the insurance money that would enable him to marry the luxury-loving Agatha is a serious inconsistency in the character of the man as he is presented throughout the story. A similar inconsistency is apparent in the strong and self-sufficient de Lhoseta who allows himself to remain for years at the mercy of Mrs. Harrington.

Through many of the situations in this book one can see reflections of the author. Merriman's own infatuation with Majorca, as evidenced by many sketches that he made, colors the descriptions of that island in *Grey Lady*. Something of his own experience must have been attributed to Eve Challoner in her activities as an embryo contributor to the magazines. A reflection of the author's attitude toward the firm for which he had worked only a few years before may be found in one of the comments he makes in connection with the plot to wreck Luke's ship: "There are a lot of old fossils sitting up at Lloyd's now who are no more fit to underwrite than they are to join the heavenly choir" (301).[15] Indeed, the details regarding the attempted insurance fraud may very well have suggested themselves to Merriman during his tenure at Lloyd's.

Some of the aphorisms used in this book are moralistic; others are strongly suggestive of the witticisms of Oscar Wilde. Examples of those in the first category are "A reconciliation to be complete must be sudden. It is too delicate a thing to bear handling" (97), or, "So Eve Challoner learnt her first lesson in that school of adversity. Where some of us pass creditably, while others are ploughed, and a few—a very few—take honors" (196–197). Typical among the quips are these: "We only make use of our knowledge of woman in the study of those women with whom other men have to do" (172), and "She was young enough to believe in the vague Good that lurketh behind Evil" (276). In a slightly different vein, one that epitomizes an attitude toward women in a man's world, it is said of Eve Challoner's writing: "He knew that Eve's work was only partially good—true woman's work that might cease to flow at any moment" (223).

There are some occasional passages of dialogue that must have been designed by Merriman to satirize the attitude of his time as to the ineffable superiority of Englishmen in the general scheme of things. Just before the wreck of the *Croonah,* a field-officer aboard jumps to his feet and shouts, " 'Look here, sir! If we are in for a cyclone, I trust that we know how to behave as men— and die as men, if need be! But don't let us have any whispering in corners, like a lot of schoolgirls. We are in the care of good men, and all we have to do is to obey orders, and—damn it, sir! —to remember we're Englishmen!' " (288).

The *Athenaeum* praised the characterizations in the book, but found the good characters less interesting than the "worldly" Agatha or the "reprehensible Mrs. Harrington."[16] The reviewer concludes that the author's sense of humor prevents his melodramatic tendencies from injuring an otherwise excellent literary work. The *Literary Weekly* is at first equally complimentary, pointing out that *The Grey Lady* has "enough freshness and vivacity to distinguish it from the rank and file of fiction."[17] This same journal revised its opinion rather sharply in considering a new edition of *The Grey Lady* in 1898. The author is accused of describing the incidents of the plot "without a trace of the ability of which he has shown himself capable in handling a dramatic situation." [18] Much in the satirical vein of Merriman himself, the reviewer offers the opinion, in respect to the new edition, that "With some novels, as with some women, it is the gown that makes the impression." [19]

V The Sowers

The Sowers, published in 1896, was Merriman's most financially successful novel. The book established him in the very forefront of popularity with the reading public. It ran to twenty editions in four years and was subsequently issued by Tauchnitz in Germany.

The story which thus made its author world famous is a synthesis of several of Merriman's favorite themes. Most prominent among these is the author's exploration of the conditions contributing to the Nihilist movement in Russia. *The Sowers,* read in conjunction with two earlier works, illustrates a readily discernible progression in the author's thinking on this problem. In *Young Mistley* the reader becomes aware of the direction of Merriman's democratic sympathies although the treatment given to the theme is tentative and inconclusive. The Nihilist protagonists, Marie and Ivan, are themselves somewhat confused as to which side they are on.

Self-interest seems to dictate the actions both of those who are in favor of the Czarist regime and of those who are opposed to it. *Prisoners and Captives* underscores the quixotic aspects of attempts to assist those who seek to escape the Russian tyranny and the general hopelessness of their tragic situation. In *The Sowers,* the author makes his position perfectly clear by becoming an outspoken champion of the purposes of the Nihilists in Russia although he deprecates their methods. Nor is his view of the situation clouded by any misty idealism in respect to the nature of the Russian peasants. Despite their conditioned brutality, he, like his hero, Prince Paul Alexis, speaks eloquently for the alleviation of their suffering, as in the following passage:

Those Nihilists, with their mysterious ways and their reprehensible love of explosives, have made honest men's lives a burden to them."

"Their motives were originally good," put in Paul. "That is possible; but a good motive is no excuse for a bad means. They wanted to get along too quickly. They are pig-headed, exalted, unpractical to a man. I do not mention the women, because when women meddle in politics they make fools of themselves, even in England. These Nihilists would have been all very well if they had been content to sow for posterity. But they wanted to see the fruits of their labors in one generation. Education does not grow like that. It requires a couple of generations to germinate. It has to be manured by the brains of fools before it is of any use. In England it has reached this stage; here in Russia the sowing has only begun. Now, we were doing some good. The Charity League was the thing. It began by training their starved bodies to be ready for the education when it came. And very little of it would have come in our time. If you educate a hungry man, you set a devil loose upon the world. Fill their stomachs before you feed their brains, or you will give them mental indigestion; and a man with mental indigestion raises hell or cuts his own throat   (15).[20]

The character of Prince Paul illustrates the author's pervasive concern with the sense of duty which is the ruling precept in his code of ethics. Like so many of Merriman's heroes, Paul is motivated by a dominating sense of responsibility and by his adherence to the code of individualism and self-reliance. Etta Bamborough, on the other hand, represents what happens to those who lack this Spartan code of responsibility. Torn by conflicting passions—greedy materialism, love, vanity, loyalty, and betrayal—she accomplished her own destruction because she never learned to balance her emotional and physical drives on the even-handed scale of duty.

The setting of this novel is truly international, shifting from London, to Russia, to Paris. There are brilliant pictures of the diplomatic and social worlds of Paris and St. Petersburg, and realistic and powerful vignettes of life on the estates of Prince Paul and Count Lanovitch at Osterno and Thors, respectively.

Educated at Eton and Cambridge, Prince Paul Alexis of the province of Tver in Russia, together with Karl Steinmetz, his estate steward, has taken an active interest in the health and welfare of the Russian peasants. To promote this objective, he and Steinmetz have become active in the Charity League, an organization of Russian nobles designed to alleviate the incredible living conditions of the peasants and to educate them toward an appreciation of a more democratic way of life.

This league, organized by Stepan Lanovitch, whose estate at Thors is near Paul's at Osterno, was outlawed by the Czarist government after someone had stolen the records of the league from Thors and betrayed the members to the authorities. Since Paul's name was not in these records, he was not exiled. Stepan, however, was exiled to Siberia, and only his ineffectual wife, the countess, and his plain but strong-minded daughter, Catrina, are left on the estate at Thors. Catrina, like her father, is sympathetic toward the peasants, but her mother cares only for her own comfort.

Claude de Chauxville, Etta Bamborough, Steinmetz, and Paul are present at a diplomatic reception in Paris. There Paul meets fascinating, opportunistic Etta, young widow of Sydney Bamborough, who has recently died. Claude is in love with Etta, but she determines to win Paul and the title of princess. Eventually married, Paul and Etta go to Osterno for a portion of the year, taking with them Etta's cousin, Maggie Delafield, who is herself in love with Paul. Etta's marriage comes as a great blow to the ambitious and scheming Claude and to the strong-willed but hopelessly plain Catrina, who has been in love with Paul since they were children. Steinmetz, too, disapproves of the match, for he feels that Etta does not really love Paul, but is interested only in the glamor attaching to his position.

Claude seeks vengeance against both Steinmetz and Etta, and he conspires with Vassili, a Russian diplomatic agent, to help Vassili get information about Paul's activities with the Charity League and also about Etta's activities in selling the papers of the organization to Vassili. She had received these papers from her husband, Sydney, who had stolen them from Stepan during a brief visit to Thors. It was while escaping after this theft that Sydney was killed on the steppe where his body was found and recognized by Steinmetz.

At Osterno, Paul is oblivious of Catrina's regard in his new-found happiness with Etta. Catrina is, of course, jealous of Etta, and her passionate Russian nature causes her to grow gradually almost to hate Paul. Etta is unhappy in her Russian surroundings

and fearful of what may be found out about her past; the Lano-
vitches are so close and it was in the province of Tver that she
sold the papers.

Paul pursues his usual estate activities. Particularly, he tries to
help the peasants by going about incognito as the Moscow doctor
—thus he is described by the *starost,* or mayor, who is in Paul's
confidence—in order to minister to their ills with his medical skill,
since he had taken a medical degree for precisely this purpose.
Steinmetz learns a great deal about Etta and Claude in Paris from
Stepan Lanovitch, who escapes from exile and warns him about
Etta's activities.

Through Countess Lanovitch, Claude manages an invitation to
stay at Thors. Here he proceeds to poison Catrina's mind against
Paul. Encountering Etta, he reveals his knowledge of her past,
hints at further knowledge about her husband Sydney, and seeks
thus to enlist her aid in his campaign against Paul and Steinmetz.
She repulses him, but is forced to fall in grudgingly with some of
his schemes in order to keep the knowledge of her past from Paul.

Claude advises Etta that the peasants are on the verge of rising
against Paul, whom they believe to be the typical, heartless
prince. Paul has been at pains to preserve this illusion in the
minds of the peasants so that he can remain in Russia and care
for them surreptitiously. Only by appearing cruel to them can
he allay the government's suspicions about his activity in the
Charity League. Claude asks Etta's assistance in opening a side
door in the castle when the uprising occurs so that the peasants
will be able to overrun the castle. She refuses, even though she
knows he will reveal her past. He then tells her that Sydney is
not really dead and that she is not even married to Paul. The
body of the man found on the steppe was unrecognizable after
having been dragged by his horse, and, so he says, it was not
Sydney Bamborough. This revelation forces Etta to acquiesce in
his scheme because she wants to retain her title and position.

Because of her frequent *tête à têtes* with Claude, Etta is suspected by Catrina and Steinmetz of taking part in a vulgar intrigue with him. When Steinmetz taxes her with this accusation,
she denies it. He accuses Claude; and, when Claude brags of his
power over Etta, Steinmetz horsewhips him and ejects him from
the castle in order to protect both Paul and Etta. Steinmetz then

tells Paul of Etta's past and assures Etta that her husband is really dead. Paul then confronts Etta with his knowledge and coldly tells her that she will have to live in England. She can preserve her title and he will support her, but they cannot continue to live together. She is torn between a fancied hatred and a growing respect and love for Paul.

Paul is aware of the imminent peasant uprising and tries to discover the causes. Arrangements are made for the Countess Lanovitch to live in Paris, and Paul persuades Catrina and her father to escape to America so that Stepan may avoid banishment. Before she leaves, Catrina confesses to Paul her small part in aiding Claude's schemes.

Claude has been successful in bringing the peasants to the pitch of open rebellion, and the attack does come as scheduled. The castle is surrounded, and Paul removes the women to a central room and prepares for resistance. Etta is missed, and soon the peasants are heard swarming into the house. Paul and Steinmetz meet them on the stairway and halt them momentarily by firing over their heads. Finally, the two men are driven to the inner room; and, upon Steinmetz's advice, Paul dons the disguise of the Moscow doctor. When he appears thus, Steinmetz reveals that the doctor whom the peasants adore is really Prince Paul. The peasants forget their enmity, fall at the feet of the beloved Moscow doctor, then leave the house.

After the attack is over, Steinmetz seeks Etta by the side entrance and finds her dead from a blow on the head inflicted by the inrushing peasants. Near her, his hand stretched toward her as if trying to ward off the attack on her, is the body of Claude, killed in a similar fashion. Steinmetz, Paul, and Maggie realize that Etta had betrayed the castle by opening the side door. Maggie feels that Paul has been harsh with Etta because, being strong, he could not understand a weak woman's reasons for such double-dealing. Steinmetz and Paul realize that they will now be exiled from Russia because Paul has had to reveal his sympathy with the peasants by exposing himself as the Moscow doctor.

In England three years later, Steinmetz meets Maggie and tells her that Paul is presently staying with him in retirement nearby. Although they cannot return to Russia, they are still seeking to help the peasants and carry on their work as "sowers" by corre-

spondence and through agents. Maggie's feelings toward Paul
have altered, and their meeting leads to a new and happier
romance.

Perhaps more than most of Merriman's books, *The Sowers* is
filled with numerous short, incisive descriptive passages. Particularly impressive in this respect are two pictures of the countryside near Prince Paul's estate:

The moon was just rising over the line of the horizon. All around them
the steppe lay in grim and lifeless silence. In such a scene, where life
seemed rare and precious, death gained in its power of inspiring fear.
It is different in crowded cities, where an excess of human life seems
to vouch for the continuity of the race, where, in a teeming population,
one life more or less seems of little value. The rosy hue of sunset was
fading to a clear green, and in the midst of a cloudless sky, Jupiter—
very near the earth at that time—shone intense, and brilliant like a
lamp. It was an evening such as only Russia and the great North Lands
ever see, where the sunset is almost in the north and the sunrise holds
it by the hand. Over the whole scene there hung a clear, transparent
night, green and shimmering, which would never be darker than an
English twilight.

. . . .

Ahead of them a few lights twinkled feebly, sometimes visible and then
hidden again as they rode over the rolling hillocks. One plain ever suggests another, but the resemblance between the steppes of Tverland
and the great Sahara is at times startling. There is in both that roll as
of the sea—the great roll that heaves unceasingly round the Capes of
Good Hope and Horn. Looked at casually, Tver and Sahara's plains are
level, and it is only in crossing them that one realizes the gentle up and
down beneath the horses' feet   (13 ff.).

In a later passage, he uses the description of an ice party near
St. Petersburg as a penetrating analogy for the Russian character:

It was quite dark. A young moon was rising over the city, throwing out
in dark relief against the sky a hundred steeples and domes. The long,
thin spire of the Fortress Church—the tomb of the Romanoffs—shot up
into the heavens like a dagger. Near at hand a thousand electric lights
and colored lanterns, cunningly swung on the branches of the pines,
made a veritable fairyland. The ceaseless song of the skates, on ice as
hard as iron, mingled with the strains of a band playing in a kiosk with

[70]

open windows. From the ice-hills came the swishing scream of the iron runners down the terrific slope. The Russians are a people of great emotions. There is a candor in their recognition of the needs of the senses which does not obtain in our self-conscious nature. These strangely constituted people of the North—a budding nation, a nation which shall some day overrun the world—are easily intoxicated. And there is a deliberation about their methods of seeking this enjoyment which appears at times almost brutal. There is nothing more characteristic than the ice-hill   (200).

The author's ability to weigh the advantages and disadvantages of the rampant republicanism that was making its influence felt in Russia, as well as in Europe generally, is deftly demonstrated in the two passages quoted below. In the first, Merriman states the problem; in the second, he points out the consequences of the indicated solution. His own feeling that such a development, however disruptive, is necessary and inescapable is clearly apparent. The current world situation documents the accuracy of his prophecy.

Education is a dangerous matter to deal with; England is beginning to find this out for herself. For on the heels of education socialism ever treads. When at last education makes a foothold in Russia, that foothold will be on the very step of the autocratic throne. The Charity League had, as Steinmetz put it, the primary object of preparing the peasant for education, and thereafter placing education within his reach. Such proceedings were naturally held by those in high places to be only second to Nihilism   (31).

. . . .

With us in England the poor man raises up his voice and cries aloud when he wants something. He always wants something—never work, by the way—and therefore his voice pervades the atmosphere. He has his evening newspaper, which is dear at the moderate sum of a halfpenny. He has his professional organizers, and his Trafalgar Square. He even has his members of Parliament. He does no work, and he does not starve. In his generation the poor man thinks himself wise. In Russia, however, things are managed differently. The poor man is under the heel of the rich. Some day there will be in Russia a Terror, but not yet. Some day the moujik will erect unto himself a rough sort of guillotine, but not in our day. Perhaps some of us who are young men now may dimly read in our dotage of a great upheaval beside which the Terror of France will be tame and uneventful. Who can tell? When a country begins to grow its mental development is often startlingly rapid (76–77).

In *The Sowers,* as in most of his books, Merriman's comments on women and love reveal a curious mixture of idealism and cynicism. Of love he says: "There are a thousand shades of blue, and the outer shades are at last not blue at all, but green or purple. So in love there are a thousand shades, and very, very few of them are worthy of the name" (35). His hero, Paul, however, "was old-fashioned enough to look upon women as higher and purer than men, while equally capable of thought and self-control" (343). His attitude toward femininity in women is made no less clear in this novel than in his others. Disapprobation of the "bluestocking" is frequently apparent in such observations as "A learned woman is not of much account in the world. A clever woman moves as much of it as lies in her neighborhood—that is to say, as much as she cares to rule. For women love power, but they do not care to wield it at a distance" (61).

Despite the fact that reviewers sometimes accused Merriman of not understanding the intricacies of women,[21] his comment in *The Sowers* in respect to beauty versus plainness in women reveals a perception of the female nature not often found in the typical romantic novel: "Men are in the habit of forgetting that plain women are women at all. Surely some of them may be excused for reminding us at times that they are also capable of loving—that they also desire to be loved. Happy is the man who loves and is loved of a plain woman; for she will take her own lack of beauty into consideration, and give him more than most beautiful women have it in their power to give" (114).[22]

The author's healthily cynical view of the social foibles of his day is evidenced by the serio-comic understatements with which he lampoons cultural hypocrisy, insincerity, and organized charity. Concerning the first of these, he says, with more than a hint of Dickens in his proper names,

Of course, M. de Chauxville knew that Lady Mealhead had once been the darling of the music-halls, and that a thousand hearts had vociferously gone out to her from sixpenny and even threepenny galleries when she answered to the name of Tiny Smalltoes. Nor could M. de Chauxville take exception at young Cyril Squyrt, the poet. Cyril looked like a poet. He wore his hair over his collar at the back, and below the collar-bone in front. And, moreover, he was a poet—one of those who write for the ages yet unborn   (20–21).

Concerning Catrina's refreshing forthrightness, he admonishes that

It must be remembered in extenuation that Catrina Lanovitch had lived nearly all her life in the province of Tver. She was not modern at all. Deprived of the advantages of our enlightened society press, without the benefit of our decadent fictional literature, she had lamentably narrow views of life. She was without that deep philosophy which teaches you, mademoiselle, who read this guileless tale, that nothing matters very much; that love is but a passing amusement, the plaything of an hour; that if Tom is faithless, Dick is equally amusing; while Harry's taste in gloves and compliments is worthy of some consideration   (110).

Merriman never lost an opportunity to fire a blast at one of his favorite targets—the charity "schemes" which were as prevalent then as now. Unalterably opposed to such organized giving, he conceived of true charity in the Biblical sense, as is evident from this passage: "This is an age of societies, and, far from concealing from the left hand the good which the right hand may be doing, we publish abroad our charities on all hands. We publish in a stout volume our names and donations. We even go so far as to cultivate an artificial charity by meat and drink and speeches withal" (62).

Scattered throughout the book are numerous revelations of the author's attitudes in respect to such themes as vanity, publicity, the Jewish race, realism, and the natural supremacy of nobility. The vain and luxury-loving Etta is described as turning around before an admiring audience "like a beautifully garnished joint before the fire of cheap publicity" (146). Of a minor character in the book Merriman observes: "He had Jewish blood in his veins, which . . . carried with it the usual tendency to cringe. It is in the blood; it is part of what the people who stood without Pilate's palace took upon themselves and upon their children" (86–87). Vis-à-vis romance versus realism, he presents the usual argument that "romance serves to elevate, while realism tends undoubtedly toward deterioration" (118). When Paul and Steinmetz are holding the peasants at bay in the castle at Osterno, the author speaks out on the side of birth: "Two men holding a hundred in check! But one of them was a prince, which makes all the difference, and will continue to make that difference, despite halfpenny journalism, until the end of the world" (371).

The Sowers was widely and, for the most part, favorably reviewed. The *Saturday Review* calls it the best of the earlier books of Merriman "all of which display a genuine talent for story telling." [23] The reviewer then calls the book intellectually torpid because it is aimed at the common level. Because the book shows a "ridiculous concept of Russian social structures," the reviewer doubts that Merriman was ever inside Russia, despite the fact that the story was received in England as an "instructive study of social and political conditions." [24] Steinmetz and de Chauxville are described as marionettes "jerked vigorously about."

The *Athenaeum* subscribes to the opinion that Steinmetz is an imperfectly realized character, but speaks highly of the book's strength and freshness. Prince Paul is described as being admirably drawn, and comment is made as to the poetry and imagination displayed by the author's "subtle suggestions of the similarity of his sturdy character to the vast forests around his estates." [25] The chief objection by this reviewer is aimed at the author's self-conscious asides and cynical reflections.

Helena J. Albro in the American *Bookman* calls the story a "vividly written romance of Russian life, with a cleverly constructed plot that keeps the interest keenly alive." [26] She praises the author's "freshness of thought and piquancy of expression." Conflicting, as it does, with the *Athenaeum* reviewer's opinion, this last statement illustrates that such criticism is largely a matter of a personal rather than an objective response.

The *Academy*[27] and the *Critic*[28] were both largely complimentary in their reviews, although the former found fault with Merriman's arithmetic when he described an area of two hundred square miles as presenting a vista "suggestive of immense distance, of countless miles in all directions." Both Paul and Steinmetz are referred to by the *Academy* as interesting, lovable characters.

VI Flotsam

The publication of *Flotsam,* also in 1896, marked a new emphasis in technique for Merriman. Although it is essentially a story of the Indian Mutiny, it is his only book in which plot is subservient to character analysis. According to Elwin, *Flotsam* "illustrates the psychological conception that shows how a strain of weakness in the brilliantly gifted Harry Wylam created tragedy for himself and sorrow and suffering for all around him." [29] In this respect, the book follows the classical pattern of Aristotelian tragedy. In *Flotsam* and, to a lesser extent, in *The Phantom Future,* Merriman exemplifies the design, noted as applicable to his work by Elwin, of applying "to popular romance the principles of psychology and refinement advocated and practised by Henry James and W. D. Howells." [30]

In his tribute to Merriman in the London *Times,* Oliver Edwards comments on the interesting departure which *Flotsam* marks in the author's fictional methods.

But for myself I have always put one book of Merriman's in a class by itself. In thirteen volumes Merriman is a story-writer. In *Flotsam* he became a novelist proper. Merriman himself subtitled it "The Study of a Life" and that is what it is. Harry Wylam's tragedy was born with him; it was in his character. There is no happy ending to the love story of Harry and Miriam or to Harry's life; the book closes none the less with a certain sense of fulfillment. Ill-starred a man may be, but he can reach the farther shore at last.[31]

Although this detailed study of the complete disintegration of character under the impetus of evil counsel seems at first glance to be a radical new direction for Merriman, it is not really so. Most of his books celebrate the strong, heroic figure whose actions are guided by self-reliance and a sense of responsibility. In *Flotsam* the author chooses to show the consequences, in terms of human suffering, when the protagonist lives outside this code. The cause of Harry Wylam's downfall is his willingness to sacrifice principles to greed and the desire for position.

Merriman had shown us this picture before, with some minor modifications; and he was to do it again. Tom Valliant in *The Phantom Future* illustrates the uselessness of life without a guiding purpose, as do Alfred Huston in *The Grey Lady* and Geoffrey Horner in *In Kedar's Tents*. These three are afraid to face life because they have no real reason for living. Another group of Merriman's characters are led to disaster or near it, either because they have no goal in life or because they succumb to the temptation of choosing an unworthy goal. These include Luke Fitz-Henry and Agatha Ingham-Baker in *The Grey Lady*, Percy Roden in *Roden's Corner*, The Vicomte de Clericy in *Dross*, and Loo Barebone in *The Last Hope*. Then there are a number of characters, each of whom has some incipiently admirable qualities, who deliberately orient themselves to evil practices from motives of self-aggrandizement. Among these are Seymour Michael in *From One Generation to Another*, Victor Durnovo in *With Edged Tools*, Mrs. Harrington in *The Grey Lady*, Claude de Chauxville in *The Sowers*, Phillip Lamond in *Flotsam*, Otto Von Holzen in *Roden's Corner*, and Colonel Gilbert in *The Isle of Unrest*. At least two of these—Durnovo and Von Holzen—are highly intriguing tenants of a fictional rogues' gallery.

Harry Wylam of *Flotsam* belongs to the second of the three categories outlined above. The story of his misadventures begins with Harry as a boy being brought from his home in India to the London home of his cousin and potential guardian, John Gresham, a wealthy shipowner. Young Harry's parents have recently died in India of cholera, and since then he has lived with Phillip Lamond, formerly his father's agent. Lamond wishes to remain as guardian to Harry chiefly, it is learned, because he is interested in getting control of the boy's inheritance.

Harry is delivered to the care of Mr. Gresham by Captain Farr, the captain of Gresham's ship, *The Golden Horn*. In Gresham's home, Harry is treated kindly but firmly; he learns to play with and admire Miriam Gresham, the small daughter of the household. By the time he is ready for school, he has already begun to assert his superiority as an Englishman and a gentleman. When attempts are made to curb his childish tyranny, he runs away to become a sailor, but he is rescued and returned to London by Mr. Gresham's butler, Parks. The boy is then sent to military school where he eventually obtains his commission. Upon returning to his guardian's house, he finds that Miriam has grown into a beautiful young lady. He declares his love for her, but his guardian puts him off for two years.

Harry comes into his inheritance when he reaches his twenty-fifth birthday, and at a party with his regiment celebrating this occasion, he challenges his brother officer, Montague, to a duel because of a disrespectful remark Montague makes about Miriam when he is drunk. Although Gresham forbids Harry both his daughter and his house if he fights the duel, Harry goes through with it and wounds Montague in the neck. Outraged, Harry's major tells him he will have to leave the regiment and the country.

Montague recovers, but Harry is slated to go to India. Before his departure, he writes a letter of contrition to Mr. Gresham. Miriam answers the letter, telling Harry her father is ill. Although forbidden to do so, Harry goes to see Miriam and acquaints her with the reason for the duel. Upon learning this, Miriam pledges herself to wait all her life for Harry, if need be.

In India, Harry and Lamond meet again, and Harry is greatly attracted by Lamond's opportunistic daughter, Maria. He is encouraged in this attraction by Lamond, who also abets Harry's evident intention to ruin himself by gambling. When the Indian Mutiny breaks out, Lamond betrays battle plans of the English to the Indian mutineers. He involves Harry in his duplicity by persuading the young man to join him in blowing up and looting an Indian temple. Harry is motivated to do so by his desire to recoup his fortune.

Fred Marqueray, a captain in Wylam's Indian regiment, is in reality a secret-service officer for the British. In an attempt to discover how the battle plans were betrayed to the enemy, Marqueray disguises himself as a fakir and goes behind the Indian battle lines in Delhi. He discovers Lamond's guilt, but he is seen and recognized in his disguise by Wylam. Later, Lamond deduces that it must be Marqueray who has been following him so sedulously in the guise of a fakir.

Harry is slightly wounded, but upon recovery he soon dissipates his share of the money obtained in the raid on the temple. In the depths, of despair at his imminent ruin, Harry attempts to shoot himself; but he is prevented by Lamond who intimates that Maria is in love with Harry. He entices Wylam into signing over his rights to his Indian property by promising to set the young couple up in housekeeping should they decide to marry.

Lamond sends money to Harry and Maria, who are now married and the parents of a daughter. When Harry tries to borrow additional money, his banker reveals that only half Harry's income had been sent to England. The other half, by order of his father, had been accruing in a Delhi bank—to the extent of two million rupees. Harry learns that Lamond knew of this sum and realized why Lamond had made him sign over his rights to all his Indian property. He faces Lamond with his knowledge of this thievery and reveals Lamond's villainy to all the members of an exclusive Indian club. Lamond in turn accuses Harry publicly of being solely responsible for the Delhi explosion to enrich himself with the treasure from the temple. To the same gathering Marqueray reveals that Lamond is a spy.

Harry is placed under military arrest. Lamond and his daughter flee from India, taking Harry's child with them. Lamond has seen to it, meanwhile, that Harry's property is settled on Maria.

The court-martial resulting from his involvement in the temple raid does not find Harry guilty. Marqueray advises him to get back his child from Maria and to take the child to Miss Gresham in England. Harry retrieves the child and takes her to England, where Miriam Gresham agrees to care for her. Harry then returns to Cape Town where he works as a teamster; there he falls seriously ill and dies, as futilely as he had lived.

The plot of *Flotsam*, although of secondary interest, is an adequate vehicle for the extended character analysis which supplies the major interest. Although there is less of Merriman in this book because of the objective nature of the writing, some characteristic touches are included from time to time. For example, the author naturally champions the imperialistic motive behind the Indian Mutiny and England's war with Russia, which was being waged at the same time. He does, however, offer the opinion that the Indian governor general, Lord Canning, might have avoided open conflict in India if he had handled the native situation more wisely. At the same time, Merriman is fully cognizant of the opportunistic view of the war taken by the English populace. "In England," he says wryly, "the war was popular. We are shopkeepers, my masters. Let us admit that" (108).[32] His opinion of the individuals composing the society which could thus turn tragedy to advantage is indicated in such a typical aphorism as "If a dog be given a bad name, nowadays, he usually gets into society with it" (13). Fortunately for England and for Merriman, however, there were such dedicated people as Miriam Gresham and Wylam's colonel, "a man of the quality that has brought a certain small island of the north to the front rank of nations" (99).

The conception of the character of Harry Wylam indicates, as did Father Max Talma in *The Slave of the Lamp,* some influences from Thackeray. There are some points of similarity between Wylam and Rawdon Crawley of *Vanity Fair,* but the resemblance to the hero of Thackeray's *Barry Lyndon* is too close to be accidental. While she is not so completely realized, the adventuress Maria Lamond is an amoral sister to Becky Sharp.

Significantly, Merriman's critics seem to have missed the psychological basis of the book. It remained for Malcolm Elwin, and later Oliver Edwards, to point this out. Perhaps the mass of readers and reviewers of Merriman's own time were not conditioned to accepting the unpleasant realism of the author's presentation of a weak-willed but pitiable figure. The *Academy* says that Merriman "has not created a better character than. . . . Harry Wylam," [33] but he calls Wylam a "sport of the fates," whereas Harry's tragedy grows from within rather than from without.

The *Academy* also points out certain improbabilities in the character of Phillip Lamond. These are made more explicit by the *Athenaeum,* which questions how a known traitor in India could appear later as "the member of an exclusive London club" [34] and as a general of Indian forces. This reviewer notes Wylam's resemblance to Rawdon Crawley. The *Saturday Review* also notes the similarity between Wylam and Barry London and comments on Merriman's evident familiarity with the Indian scene, but finds the hero a totally unsympathetic "mindless bully, gambler, and blackguard." [35] Lamond too is found to be unconvincing, and both *Flotsam* and *The Sowers* are judged to be "far below" Merriman's "earlier and better books."

VII In Kedar's Tents

Merriman's amazing productivity is attested by the fact that the year 1896 marked the publication of a volume of character sketches, *The Money Spinner*—a cooperative effort between him and his sister-in-law—in addition to two of his major works, *The Sowers* and *Flotsam*. The very next year saw yet another novel, *In Kedar's Tents,* generally adjudged to be one of his best. Elwin, for instance, lists this novel—along with *The Velvet Glove, The Vultures, Barlasch of the Guard, The Sowers,* and *With Edged Tools* —as "the best of Merriman." [36] Swinnerton calls *In Kedar's Tents* the "most exciting of all his [Merriman's] stories." [37] Edward Wagenknecht, however, gives brief attention to *In Kedar's Tents* as one of Merriman's "best known titles." [38] In estimating Merriman's total contribution, Oliver Edwards says that he "was not likely to have bettered *In Kedar's Tents, The Velvet Glove, Flotsam,* and *The Sowers*." [39]

Basically, *In Kedar's Tents,* is an exploration of the excesses of radicalism—among the Chartists in England and the Carlists in Spain—and the suffering engendered by such excesses. Merriman is firmly on the side of evolution as opposed to revolution in respect to social and political reform. Speaking through Prince Paul in *The Sowers,* he asserts his conviction that Nihilism should have been content to sow for posterity rather than to demand the fruits of its labors in one generation. Furthermore, he stipulates that education for change is slow, both in germination and growth. *In Kedar's Tents* is a reiteration and elaboration of such beliefs transferred to his own country and to Spain.

The story accords equal emphasis to the theme of the necessity, in terms of accomplishment, of unwavering devotion to duty; and several characters illustrate it. Sir John Pleydell is relentless in the pursuit of the individual responsible for his son Alfred's death in a Chartist uprising until he learns that Frederick Conyngham had taken the blame for this death upon himself in a misguided effort to save his friend Horner who was really the guilty party. General Vincente follows the path of duty even when it leads him to act against his better judgment. Father Concha is a refreshing study of a simple priest whose actions are governed always by his loyalty to his church and to those he loves. Equally admirable in this respect is the gentle and beautiful Estella Vincente. Even Esteban Larralde, intriguer that he is, acts from a genuine devotion to the Carlist faction. The greatest sacrifice, however, is made by Frederick Conyngham, whose melodramatic flair for adventure impels him to dedicate himself to a cause not his own. From an unambitious Irish lawyer, Conyngham develops, under the impetus of duty, into the typically tenacious and selfless Merriman hero of romance. The purposeless Horner and the fatuous Señora Barenna, on the other hand, represent the vacuity and helplessness of life without direction.

The action begins near Durham in the northern manfacturing district of England, against the background of the Chartist agitation. Soon the scene shifts to Spain, especially Ronda, Ciudad Real, Toledo, and Madrid, at the height of the Carlist rebellion. In a few swift strokes, the author sketches in the necessary historical data concerning these periods of unrest in England and Spain. He characterizes Chartism as a struggle for extension of the suffrage and parliamentary representation for the working classes of England through abolition of property qualifications. In respect to the Spanish situation, he records how Ferdinand VII of Spain had bequeathed his kingdom to his daughter Isabella in defiance of the Salic Law, by which women were excluded from inheriting the throne. Ferdinand's brother, Don Carlos, however, claimed the throne as the rightful heir, contending that the Salic Law had never been legally abrogated. Don Carlos' supporters were eventually defeated.

Geoffrey Horner, a gentleman radical, has become a Chartist through a desire to get even with a world which refuses to recognize his superior attainments. At a meeting of the group near Durham, the members make an attack on the home of Sir John Pleydell, a wealthy manufacturer. Windows in the Pleydell house are smashed, and Pleydell's son, Alfred, leads a counterattack on the group. In the ensuing melee, Horner strikes Alfred a blow which subsequently causes his death. No one having seen the personal encounter between Horner and Alfred, Horner escapes; and later he tells his story to his friend, Frederick Conyngham, a bored and briefless Irish lawyer in London.

Motivated apparently by friendship for Horner and by a desire to break the monotony of his own life, Conyngham persuades Horner, without much difficulty, to allow him to assume the responsibility for whatever consequences may result from Horner's guilt. When the news of Alfred's death appears, Conyngham escapes to Spain, leaving behind him clues that indicate that Conyngham, and not Horner, is the man sought by the authorities in the Pleydell case. Horner cravenly accepts his friend's sacrifice and thenceforth disappears from the story.

Conyngham arrives in Spain with a letter of introduction to General Vincente, from whom he hopes to get a commission in the Spanish Royalist forces. In Spain, he meets Esteban Larralde, who, learning that Conyngham is going to Ronda, asks him to deliver a pink-tinted letter, described as a love note, to a certain Señorita Julia Barenna. In Ronda, Conyngham is received kindly by General Vincente and his daughter Estella. It is apparent that Conyngham and Estella have fallen in love at first sight. Julia Barenna, Estella's cousin, and Julia's mother call at the Vincentes'; and Conyngham gives Larralde's note to Julia. This action is noted by both General Vincente and the mayor, who, suspecting political activity, presses Julia about the letter. Flustered by the mayor's questioning, Julia, in front of Estella and her father, tells the mayor that the letter is a love note from Conyngham. With gentlemanly courtesy, Conyngham acquiesces in Julia's deception, although he knows that Estella must be bitterly disappointed in him.

Vincente gives Conyngham a letter to General Espartero in Madrid, in which he recommends him to Espartero's staff, and Conyngham sets out with the rascally peasant, Concepcion Vara, as guide. Himself a smuggler, Vara is bitter about all authority and law, feeling that the country would be better off without the *guardia civile*.

Julia has meanwhile returned the letter to Conyngham with instructions to give it to Colonel Monreal of Xeres. Though Monreal is not at home, Conyngham leaves the letter on his table; by now he suspects that it is not a simple love letter. He then despatches Vara back to Ronda to tell Julia that the letter has been delivered. Unknown to Conyngham, however, Monreal has been assassinated and his servant Sebastian has stolen all his papers, including the letter, because Sebastian knows that Monreal is a Carlist and he hopes to sell the papers at a profit to the Royalists. Father Concha, Julia's confessor, learns these details while following along after Conyngham and trying to trace the letter in an effort to extricate Julia from her political entrapment. Concha even tries unsuccessfully to buy the letter from Sebastian.

Larralde, who has grown suspicious as to how much Conyngham knows about the letter, waylays him along the road, believing that Conyngham has stolen the letter for himself, since it had not turned up among Monreal's effects. Larralde stabs Conyngham and flees. Having been found and taken to a hospital by some good Samaritans, Conyngham does not reach Madrid for more than six weeks. Conyngham's failure to appear in Madrid causes General Vincente to doubt him. When Conyngham finally does encounter the Vincentes, now in Madrid to be near Queen Christina in a protective capacity, and tells what has happened to him, Estella informs him that she will trust him only if he shows her the letter he gave to Julia.

Sir John Pleydell now appears unexpectedly in Madrid, seeking to extradite and prosecute the man responsible for his son's death. He has learned that Conyngham may know something of this man, and Conyngham daringly tells Pleydell that he himself is the killer.

Larralde finally obtains the letter from Sebastian. He forces Julia to inform Conyngham that she has the letter and will give it to him to show to Estella if he will come to her in Toledo. Having been hired by Pleydell to help trace his son's murderer, Larralde plans to ambush Conyngham and to get rid of him as one dangerous to the Carlist cause.

Vara gets two troopers from General Vincente in order to rescue Conyngham from the carriage in which he is being transported to the Spanish border where, as the result of an agreement between Larralde and Pleydell, he will be received and taken back to England by Pleydell. The rescue is accomplished, and Conyngham returns to Toledo where he meets Pleydell. Pleydell cannot help admiring Conyngham and he finally divines that Conyngham is not the man he seeks, but is, in fact, shielding someone else. He faces Conyngham with this fact, and Conyngham does not deny it. Pleydell concludes that whoever Conyngham is shielding must be a wonderful person to inspire such a sacrifice, and he says that he may not seek the individual farther; but he warns Conyngham against Larralde. Later, he tells the Vincentes that he had been mistaken in accusing Conyngham of attacking his son. In order to make reparations to Conyngham, Pleydell makes a bargain with Larralde for £200 to borrow the letter so that Conyngham can show it to Estella.

Julia reveals to Concha that the letter really contains details of a Carlist attack to be made on the Queen Regent. It was passed from person to person by messenger because the plotters did not trust the mails. The attack—to be made when the Queen Regent arrives in Madrid from Seville to rejoin her daughter, the Queen —is to be a signal for an uprising all over Spain.

General Vincente meets the Queen Regent in Ciudad Real and sends her incognita by a roundabout way to Madrid. He dresses Estella like the Queen, and they take the royal coach the direct way to Madrid. Father Concha goes with them in the carriage, and Conyngham and Vara act as guards; though Vincente does not approve of the morals of the Queen, he arranges this plan because of a sense of duty. An attack on the carriage along the way is beaten off. Arrived in Toledo, Vincente's group lodges in one of the royal dwellings, which is soon attacked by the mob. Vincente, Concha, Conyngham, Vara, and some of the guards sally out to beat off the attackers. The mob disperses, but Vincente is killed. Some time after these events, Conyngham returns to Ronda with the letter. He gives it to Estella, but she tears it into small pieces, saying she never really wanted it, and Conyngham has his reward.

The book reveals some clues to Merriman's reading and the influence it had on his own narrative techniques. The parallel between the self-sacrifice of Conyngham and that of Sydney Carton of Dickens' *Tale of Two Cities* is a rather obvious one. There is a slight difference, however, in the motivation of the two men. While Carton's sacrifice resulted from his hopeless love of Lucy Manette, that of Conyngham must be ascribed to his love of adventure and to his friendship for Horner. Merriman departed still further from his model in arranging a happy, rather than a tragic, conclusion to his hero's quixotism.

That the author was familiar with the pleasant reminiscences of George Borrow, the philologist author of *Lavengro* and *The Romany Rye*, is apparent from a passage of dialogue between Sir John Pleydell and Señora Barenna. Concerning her relationship to Father Concha, the Señora observes to Sir John that Father

Concha has forbidden her to buy one of the Bibles peddled by the itinerant Borrow.

Merriman's fondness for foreshadowing as a means of heightening suspense is evidenced quite early in this book. "With his [Horner's] mistakes Fate raised the curtain, and on the horizon of several lives arose a cloud no bigger than a man's hand" (3).[40]

The self-interest that often adheres to both religion and romantic love is not overlooked by the author. Queen Christina is described as "not the first to turn the strong current of man's passion to her own deliberate gain; nay, ninety-nine out of a hundred women do it. But the majority only play for a suburban villa and a few hundred pounds a year" (279). Institutional self-seeking is exemplified by Father Concha who "true to his cloth, . . . was the enemy of all progress and distrusted every innovation" (137).

One of the reviewers calls *In Kedar's Tents* a novel "suggestive of good cabinet workmanship." [41] Particularly in those portions of the story taking place in Carlist Spain, the point is well taken. One has the feeling, however, that the account of Horner's misadventures in England is a springboard designed solely to catapult the hero, Conyngham, into the thick of the Spanish rebellion. This feeling is augmented by the fact that, once the action in Spain is well under way, Horner and his difficulties are completely forgotten.

Fate also plays an important role in this story. Horner's involvement with the Chartist uprising, Conyngham's meetings with Julia Barenna, Estella, and Larralde, and the death of General Vincente—all of these incidents are fortuitous; and the tremendous consequences of the appearance and disappearance of the mysterious pink letter give to chance the same fateful importance that may be discerned again in some of Hardy's novels. Such maneuvering sometimes has the effect of sacrificing deep feeling and vital character delineation to circumstance.

Most of the notices of this widely reviewed novel agree, however, that it is a "vigorous, well constructed story with incidents following in dramatic necessity." [42] Many also note that the author's frequent epigrams sometimes conceal mere platitudes.[43] Some of the reviewers attribute a certain transitional jerkiness to the fact that the novel appeared as a serial in the *Cornhill* prior to book publication.[44]

After publication, the book was serialized in the American *Bookman*. John Lennox,[45] reviewing the story at that time, commented on the stock characters of this and other adventure stories, noting that they included the bold, bad, beautiful woman; the large young man for the lead; the astute man of the world; and the pure, cold English maiden concealing her emotions. Concha and Vara are referred to as "very much alive," and the reviewer concludes that the story would make excellent drama. Paradoxically, the reviewer for the *Academy*,[46] after referring to the book as one of the most interesting novels of recent years, compliments the author for having rid himself of qualities of staginess. He also remarks that the two main strands of the story are not tied together, and he picks out General Vincente, along with Concha and Vara, as the most striking figures in the book. The *Athenaeum*[47] places *In Kedar's Tents* even above *The Sowers* in "neatness and vigor" and emphasizes the theatrical effectiveness of both actors and action. Most of the reviews justly praise, either implicitly or explicitly, the author's careful use of history and his penetrating glimpses of social development in England and in Spain.

VIII   Roden's Corner

On the dedication page of *Roden's Corner*, which Merriman published in 1898, appears a quotation from Omar Khayyam that is applicable not only to this book but to virtually everything that Merriman wrote:

'Tis all a Chequer-board of Nights and Days
Where Destiny with men for Pieces plays:
Hither and thither moves, and mates, and slays,
And one by one back in the Closet lays.

Indeed, says Swinnerton, "For 'Destiny' read 'Henry Seton Merriman', and you define his limitations. Within those limitations he is a master." [48]

Both the social world and the business world appear as separate entities in many of Merriman's books. *Roden's Corner* presents a synthesis of these two worlds—the world of commerce superimposed on that of society. In this respect, the book combines some of the best features of the romance and of the novel of business; and Merriman established, if not a precedent, at least a rather radical departure for an erstwhile popular romancer. A hint as to the originality of his conception may be found in a reviewer's cavil that "British readers object to a commercial novel such as this masquerading as a romance. Commercial stories belong to the newspapers where the truth is stranger than this fiction." [49] An objection like this, is, of course, specious. An artist is not to be criticized on the basis that he is an innovator, but rather on the degree to which he has made his innovation plausible and credible—in this case, on the extent to which he has successfully adapted the techniques of realism to the romantic formula.

The story of *Roden's Corner* moves on two levels—the hardheaded, profit-grabbing level of corporation finance that reflects the attitude of big business toward labor in Queen Victoria's day, and the vague and visionary level of an upper class completely unsophisticated in respect to business methods and more concerned with the concept of charity than with its fruits. Entrepreneur Percy Roden and the unscrupulous Von Holzen represent business; and the willing dupe, Lord Ferriby, and his erstwhile playboy nephew, Anthony Cornish, represent society. In the juxtaposed characters of Roden and Cornish, Merriman succeeds in executing a sort of double-regeneration pattern of development. Cornish rapidly develops a social conscience and becomes a man with a purpose—an implacable avenger of the inhumanly sharp practices of his nefarious business associates in the charity schemes. Roden gradually changes from an unprincipled opportunist, dedicated solely to self-interest, to a man who is haunted by the full realization of the enormity of his exploitation of the Malgamite workers. The other principal characters—Lord Ferriby and his daughter Joan, Roden's sister Dorothy, the worldly Edith Vansittart, and that portrait of the popular conception of the heroic but inarticulate Englishman, Major White—give social and emotional depth to the events centering around the pseudocharitable Malgamite cartel. Roden, the promoter, and the coldly calculating evil genius, Von Holzen, are two of the most successfully realized figures in Merriman's entire gallery of characters.

It has been pointed out previously that Merriman was opposed to organized charity. This book is, at least in part, a justification for that opposition. The author is frequently concerned with seeking out the selfish motive behind the ostensibly generous gesture. All but two of those directly concerned in the Malgamite enterprise had a personal stake in the proceedings. Only Cornish and White were determined that the charity scheme should accomplish exactly the purpose for which it was organized—the relief of the deadly working conditions of laborers engaged in the papermaking industry. The book emphasizes the tragedy that must inevitably result from charity promulgated for gain or for the purpose of advertising to the left hand that which the right hand is doing. Often, as in this story, the professional "do-gooder" is victimized by opportunists such as Von Holzen and Roden.

The action of the story passes in the fashionable world of London, the home of Lord and Lady Ferriby; the diplomatic world of The Hague, where Mrs. Vansittart lives; and the nearby manufacturing town of Scheveningen, location of the Malgamite plant.

Von Holzen, a German chemist, buys the formula for Malgamite, an ingredient necessary to the manufacture of paper, from a worker in Holland who soon dies after selling the formula. Having obtained the formula, Von Holzen thereupon removes the purchase price from the worker's dead fingers. This laborer, like many of those engaged in the manufacture of Malgamite, dies from the effects of the dangerous carbonic acid gas used in its manufacture.

Von Holzen represents this formula to his future associates as a new and safe way of making Malgamite, a method which will save the workers from the death that formerly decimated them. Actually it is a cheaper but even more deadly method of manufacture. He interests Percy Roden, an ambitious young business manager, in forming a company to control the Malgamite market. Together, they enlist Lord Ferriby and his daughter Joan in the scheme, representing it as a charity organized for the purpose of gathering the workers from all over the world together in Scheveningen, Holland, where quarters and facilities may be built for them to carry on their trade in safety.

Lord Ferriby, an influential and pompous old man, has a finger in virtually every charity scheme. Joan is a sincere but misguided enthusiast for all her father's charities. Anthony Cornish, Ferriby's socialite nephew, is also asked to join the charity, as is Major

White, a middle-aged and very popular British war hero. All these people are recruited to lend tone and "face" to the bogus charity. Dorothy Roden, a sincere and honest girl, recognizes her brother's tendency to follow a fatal ambition, but she thinks it her duty to keep house for him and look after him.

The charity is launched and contributions begin pouring in. The manufactory is established at Scheveningen; and the Malgamite workers, most of whom are marked for death by the poisonous nature of their occupation, are assembled there under the direction of Von Holzen as manager and Roden as financier and business manager. The works are kept under close guard, and the workers are treated as prisoners under surveillance. Most of them are willing to put up with the conditions because of the promised safety and a prospective small share in the profits of the sale of Malgamite to the paper manufacturers.

Mrs. Edith Vansittart, a handsome and mysterious widow who lives alone at The Hague, arranges to meet Cornish, who is a friend of hers from the old days before she was married to her now deceased husband. She does not explain her presence in The Hague at this time. Meanwhile, Cornish, through his association with Roden, has met Dorothy, with whom he has fallen in love, despite the fact that there has been a sort of understanding that he and Joan would one day marry. Dorothy is at first not aware of Tony's personal interest, but it is plain that she reciprocates his feeling. Major White, whose façade of the hard-fighting, virtuous English soldier covers a native shrewdness, forms a silent but sincere attachment for Joan Ferriby. Roden, who meets Mrs. Vansittart at The Hague, determines to marry her in order to bolster his success and social standing. For reasons of her own, Mrs. Vansittart does not discourage him.

The paper manufacturers are forced to pay exorbitant prices for the necessary Malgamite, and they band together to break Roden's monopoly and to save themselves from ruin. The workers themselves are dying at an increased rate because of the even deadlier nature of Von Holzen's manufacturing process. When Cornish becomes aware of the public criticism of the supposed Malgamite charity, he and White determine to investigate the situation.

Joseph Wade, a London banker and family friend of the Cornishes, has hoped that Tony will marry his beautiful and flippant daughter, Marguerite, just returned from school. This Tony refuses to do because of his feelings toward Dorothy. Wade tells Tony that the Malgamite charity is a fraud—really a cover for a gigantic monopoly that not only is increasingly responsible for the high death rate among the workers, but is making huge profits for Von Holzen and Roden under the guise of charity, while slowly driving the paper manufacturers into bankruptcy. He advises Tony to get out to save his reputation, but Tony decides to stay in an attempt to defeat the wily Von Holzen and to save his pompous uncle's reputation in society. White joins him in this purpose. They seek to persuade Lord Ferriby to disassociate himself from this ignoble scheme, but Ferriby has been accepting payments from Von Holzen and refuses to believe Cornish's accusations.

Tony has told Dorothy that he loves her but that he must clean up the Malgamite situation before they can think of marriage. He tells her that he feels her brother, unlike Von Holzen, is guilty more of overweening ambition than of criminal intent.

Through Roden, Mrs. Vansittart has met Von Holzen, who seems to recognize her as the wife of Karl Vansittart, a former associate of his. She persuades Roden to take her to visit the Malgamite works; in the office (while Von Holzen and Roden are both absent) she uses a key, made from an impression of Roden's key which she had previously borrowed on a pretext, to open the office safe. She is on the point of taking Von Holzen's secret formula from the safe when he returns. When he wrests the formula from her, she reveals that she is the widow of Karl Vansittart, a former partner of his in a business venture. Some irregularities had occurred in respect to finances. Von Holzen, who had committed these irregularities, had shunted the blame to Vansittart and the stigma had caused Vansittart to commit suicide, leaving his wife well provided for but with the single-minded purpose of avenging the death of the husband whom she still loved. Von Holzen permits her to leave, but he recognizes that open warfare exists between them.

Later, Tony visits Von Holzen at the factory and accuses him of the swindle, as well as of being a murderer in purposely endangering the workers in order to make quick and easy profits. Von Holzen offers to mix some Malgamite for him, then and there, to demonstrate its harmless nature. He brings the ingredients in and, pretending to seal the stoppers, goes out for some more. Tony is almost overcome by the fumes, purposely released from the bottles. He is saved by falling against the door which is thus pushed open.

At a joint meeting of the paper manufacturers and Cornish, Ferriby, and White, one of the manufacturers accuses Ferriby of accepting money to cover up the fraud of the Malgamite charity. This public revelation so shocks Ferriby that he falls dead, a result which spells the beginning of the end for the Malgamite scheme.

Soon afterward, Von Holzen plans an ambush to have Cornish killed on the dunes outside the plant by the Malgamite workers whom he has succeeded in inciting against Cornish. Dorothy gets word of this plan through her friendship with one of the Malgamiters. She warns White of the plot; then she, Mrs. Vansittart, and White hide on the dunes and succeed in ambushing the ambushers. Thus White gets a chance to "thump" the opposition—his favorite method of settling such difficulties; and he and Tony succeed in dispersing the attackers.

In a final gesture, Von Holzen plans another attack on Cornish. Roden, having had a change of heart, is being aided in getting out of his difficulties by Cornish, who decides to help Roden for the sake of his sister, believing that he is guilty only because of his ambition, and that he did not really know the dangers of the Malgamite process or the extent of the charity swindle. He meets Roden, at Roden's request, at night by the bank of the canal near Scheveningen. Von Holzen appears out of the dark and attacks Tony with a knife. Tony eludes him, but the momentum of Von Holzen's attack causes him to topple headfirst into the canal where he drowns.

Meanwhile, Roden has proposed to Mrs. Vansittart and has been refused. With Cornish's help, he leaves the country by boat late at night. The paper manufacturers take over control of the Malgamite plant after it has been practically destroyed by the maddened workers in reaction to the knowledge that they have been swindled by Von Holzen. Those who wish to leave are paid in shares of the profits, as are those who remain.

White and Joan decide to marry. Cornish and Dorothy, who have remained behind, meet on the dunes outside Scheveningen and their meeting is blessed, bravely but wryly, by Marguerite Wade who has herself long been in love with Tony.

Roden's Corner contains numerous comments on the nature and aims of organized charity. Many of these reflect, in respect to English society, the Humanism immanent in Arnold's "Wragg is in custody" in his essay on "The Function of Criticism at the Present Time." The superficial regard of the upper classes for the suffering of the poor is satirized forcefully in Joan Ferriby's observation: "Oh, it is a splendid charity!" she answered, "Tony will tell you all about it. It is an association of which the object is to induce people to give up riding on Saturday afternoons, and to lend their bicycles to haberdashers' assistants who cannot afford to buy them for themselves. Papa is patron" (17).[50]

In the same vein, the author himself points out later that "Charity, as all the world knows, should begin at an 'at home.' Lord Ferriby knew as well as any that there are men, and perhaps even women, who will give largely in order that their names may appear largely and handsomely in the select subscription-lists" (22).

Lord Ferriby, whose charity is motivated entirely by a desire to feed his own ego, is epitomized as the professional "do-gooder," convinced that all's right with his world and desiring only a prominent place on the subscription lists: "The world is full of people who will not give money, but offer readily enough what they call their 'time' to a good cause. Lord Ferriby was lavish with his 'time,' and liked to pass it in hearing the sound of his own voice" (29).

The time-wasting futility of upper-class society is made quite clear in this description of Anthony Cornish's pursuits before he was shocked into positive action by the Malgamite swindle: "It happened to be a wire-puzzle winter, and Cornish had the best collection of rings on impossible wire mazes and glass beads strung upon intertwisted hooks in Westminster, if not, indeed, in the whole of London. Then, of course, there were the committee meetings—that is to say, the meeting of the lady committees of the bazaar, and ball sub-committees" (69).

In this novel, as in his others, Merriman displays facility in satirical observations. Many of these are ironically witty in the tradition of Oscar Wilde; most of them also exhibit considerable adroitness in probing the vagaries of human nature. Of Mrs.

Courteville he says that "she was just at that age when she did not look it—at an age, moreover, when some women seem to combine a maximum of experience with a minimum of thought" (74). Another character is described with uncomfortable finality as one who "had to be elected to the floor committee because he was Mrs. Courteville's brother and Mrs. Courteville was the best chaperon in London" (74).

Merriman's descriptions of places are generally meticulous and poetic. Occasionally, he is able, by the application of a figure of speech, to give the reader a point of reference which actually places him within the scene being described. Holland is treated thus in the following passage: "For Holland suggests to the inquiring mind an elderly gentleman, now getting a little stout, who, after a wild youth, is beginning to appreciate the blessings of repose and comfort; who, having laid by a small sufficiency, sits peaceably by the fire and reflects upon the days that are no more" (78).

He was no less adept at interpreting peoples than places. His genuine understanding of the basic nature of his own countrymen and countrywomen, whether of high or low degree, is evident in such asides as the following:

Benjamin, like most of his countrymen, considered that if one speaks English in a loud, clear voice, and adds "comprenny" rather severely, as indicating the intention of standing no nonsense, the previous remarks will translate themselves miraculously in the hearer's mind (177).

. . . .

His attitude towards the world seemed to say, "Leave me alone and I will not trouble you," which is, after all as satisfactory an attitude as may be desired. It is, at all events, better than the exchange of confidences, which leads to the barter of two valueless commodities (3).

. . . .

A woman never really loves a man until she has made him the object of a creed. And it is only the man himself who can—and in the long-run usually does—make it impossible for her to adhere to her belief (261).

Merriman's own preferences in reading gave him good precedents for his preoccupation with peoples and places. Speaking of

Mr. Wade, but certainly for himself, he notes that "He [Wade] had a taste for biography, and cherished in his stout heart a fine old respect for Thackeray and Dickens and Walter Scott. Of the modern fictionists he knew nothing" (123).

Critical opinion was pretty well divided as to the wisdom of Merriman's blending social criticism with romantic fiction. The *Bookman's* attitude on this point has already been quoted. The *Athenaeum* praises the author's descriptions of the doomed Malgamite workers, "especially in a day when public attention is being turned to the unwholesome industries." [51] Merriman is further commended for his plotting, rapid action, and power of description, but he is said to be lacking in inward perception and in understanding of the subtleties and intricacies of women.

The *Outlook*[52] stresses the unusual nature of the author's choice of subject matter for a novel and the skill with which he handles it, but the *Dial*[53] finds the plot disconnected and inexpertly resolved. The *Academy* deprecates the "heavy-handed satire" in the book and finds Von Holzen "the only attractive figure in a rather dull and lifeless" [54] work. The author is chided for "abandoning romantic material in favor of hollow society and nefarious finance." He is further accused of substituting professional regularity and facility for observation and the study of life. John Kendrick Bangs,[55] writing in *Harper's*, remarks on the similarity of Merriman's manner to that of Thackeray, and he finds Von Holzen an "excellent villain."

Possibly because of its theme, *Roden's Corner* was dismissed more lightly than it should have been in its own time. In most respects, the book is equal to Merriman's best work and it deserves to be so listed. Professor Weygandt recognized the superior qualities of the book. He praised it most highly of all the author's work, calling the story "unhackneyed and interesting," the characters "clear and distinctive," the dialogue "crisp and pointed, but natural." [56]

IX   Dross

Because Merriman felt that *Dross* was beneath his standard, the story was not issued as a book in England until a collected edition of his work appeared. It was issued in Toronto in 1899.[57] There are, however, several points of interest in this story of a ne'er-do-well young man whose character is strengthened through the acceptance of responsibility and of an old man of integrity who succumbs to the promptings of self-interest and is destroyed by greed. In many of Merriman's books, one or the other of these themes is stressed. In *Dross,* he attempts to give equal emphasis to each theme; he presents both faces of the coin by combining thesis and antithesis. He also gives minor attention to the unhappiness frequently caused by the custom of arranging marriages strictly on the basis of caste and economic equality.

Much of the action takes place in Paris and on the Continent during the unrest and excitement of the last days of Napoleon III, but there are contrasting scenes in the peaceful English countryside and in London. After quarreling with his father because of his debts and his refusal to marry Isabella Gayerson, whom his father has chosen for him because of her wealth and the proximity of the Howard and Gayerson estates, Dick Howard escapes his English creditors by concealing himself in a piano case and having himself shipped to Paris by his rascally valet, Loomer. In Paris, Dick accidentally meets an old family friend, the Paris banker John Turner. While he is talking to Turner, Dick's attention is attracted to Lucille De Clericy, the vivacious daughter of the Vicomte De Clericy, an elderly financier and the owner of large estates in Provence. Turner tells Dick that the vicomte is in need of a secretary, and Dick, anxious to meet the charming Lucille, eventually obtains the position.

His duties necessitate his living in the vicomte's house. There he meets the vicomtesse, a kindly woman who takes a motherly interest in him. The vicomte, also fond of Dick, adopts a paternalistic attitude toward him. On one occasion, Dick catches a glimpse of one of the vicomte's visitors, the mysterious Charles Miste, the secretary whose place he has taken. He has not much success with his pursuit of Lucille; she seems to be flirtatious and giddy like many young women. One day he tells her he took the position to be near her because he loves her. He also reveals that he is the heir to his father's very large fortune. She responds in jest, apparently not taking him seriously.

At Lucille's first ball, Philip Gayerson, who has just arrived from England, tells the assemblage that Dick's father, who has died recently, had not forgiven Dick the final quarrel and had left him penniless. Dick returns at this time from a trip to Provence, where he has been looking after the vicomte's estates, and hears of his father's death. He leaves for England, arrives too late for the funeral, and learns that he has the use of his ancestral estate at Hopton, but can receive the inheritance only if he marries Isabella.

He returns to Paris on the eve of the outbreak of the Franco-Prussian war, which was to lead to the collapse of Napoleon III's government. Lucille treats him quite coolly because she believes he sought to deceive her with his story of a fortune that he never received. Meanwhile, she flirts quite openly with Alphonse Giraud —dandified son of the Baron Giraud, a grasping and wealthy financier—who is a suitor for Lucille's hand. In spite of this fact, a real friendship had developed between Alphonse and Dick.

Dick, who has noticed the benignant vicomte's obvious interest in money, is present when the Baron Giraud, frightened by the war scare, seeks the vicomte's advice as to how he can protect his fortune in these troubled times. The vicomte advises him to do as he has done: convert his holdings into cash and send them out of the country. As agent for this purpose, he proposes his former secretary, Charles Miste. Believing implicitly in the vicomte, Dick assures the excitable baron of the safety of this move. Shortly afterward, the baron delivers twenty million francs to be taken out of France by Miste. Some days later the vicomte gives the baron the shocking news that Miste has absconded with the baron's twenty millions, as well as with the vicomte's own fortune. The baron, claiming that he is ruined, becomes so excited at this news that he dies of a heart attack.

The vicomte, grief-stricken by the event, insists that the baron be buried from the De Clericy house, a plan to which Alphonse agrees. Dick pledges himself to hunt Miste down and try to retrieve the separate fortunes involved. The vicomte spends much time in sorrow and solitude by the baron's casket in his study; and, shortly after the baron's funeral, the vicomtesse misses her husband and finds a suicide note he has left. The river is dragged, and a body is recovered which Dick and Alphonse identify by its clothing and general appearance as the vicomte's.

Dick assumes responsibility for the welfare of Lucille and the vicomtesse. He eventually sends them to his English estate at

Hopton, near the Gayerson estate of Fairacres. Meanwhile, the war has broken out; and, Alphonse, no longer having the money to buy a commission, enlists as a common soldier. During the war and the Commune that follows, Alphonse distinguishes himself and is wounded. Dick employs an investigator named Sander to help him in his pursuit of Miste, and devotes his entire time to this purpose.

At Hopton, Lucille and Isabella soon became great friends, and it is apparent that Isabella is poisoning the minds of Lucille and of Alphonse, when he returns from the war, against Dick. She causes Lucille to feel that Dick is a liar and that his word is not to be trusted, and she insinuates to Alphonse that Dick may cheat him in the course of recovering his fortune. In fact, she says that he is not interested in recovering it at all. Dick notices this change toward him when he comes to Hopton, but he assumes it is because Lucille and Alphonse are in love and planning to marry.

He receives reports of Miste's movements through Sander. These come usually when Miste tries to cash one of the notes which had been negotiated through Turner's Paris bank when they were delivered to Miste by the vicomte. Turner and Dick have done what they can to stop payment, but the culprit is clever and is apt to turn up anywhere. Dick, receiving word of Miste's presence in Southampton, meets there a strange young woman who is seeking news of the war in her homeland, France. He later learns that this person was actually Miste in disguise.

The De Clericy women go to stay with Isabella in her town house in London. There Isabella allows the freedom of her house to a certain Mr. Devar, who is very curious about Dick's activities. He questions Dick regarding his pursuit of Miste and seeks to discredit him in the eyes of the ladies and of Alphonse. Dick suspects that Devar may be spying on him to give information about his movements to Miste. He arranges to have Turner meet Devar, and Turner recognizes him as a dishonest former clerk of his bank whom he had dismissed. Devar is thus prevented from further machinations.

Finally, word comes from Sander that Miste is in Nice trying to cash some of his notes. Dick goes there to try to capture him, and Alphonse, still slightly suspicious of Dick, goes with him. Miste tries to escape by heading over the mountains into northern Italy.

Dick and Alphonse, who follow him in a pursuit sequence that is exceptionally well described, catch up with him on a high mountain slope. There, Miste wounds Dick; and Dick, seeking to shoot him in the legs, kills him with a bullet in the heart. About half of Alphonse's fortune is found on Miste's body. While Dick hastens to Genoa to meet Sander who expects to deter there a partner of Miste's, Alphonse remains to take care of Miste's burial and the other formalities.

At Genoa, Dick finds that Sander has not yet arrived, but he learns that a steamer is shortly to sail for South America. Suspecting that Miste's confederate may be aboard, he goes to the pier just as the boat is pulling away. He is astounded to see among the passengers at the rail his old patron, the Vicomte De Clericy. The shock and his wound upset Dick so much that he faints at his hotel.

He awakens in a hospital and there pieces together what must have happened. He concludes that the vicomte, being overly fond of money, was tempted beyond his strength, when the baron's fortune was placed in his hands. He and Miste conspired to steal it. When the baron died, the vicomte filled his coffin with books, dressed the baron's body in the vicomte's clothes, and threw it in the river. Dick verifies this deduction by exhuming the casket supposedly containing the vicomte. The vicomte, of course, with his share of the spoils, had planned to start a new life in South America. Before these details are all worked out, Dick is told in the hospital that the South American ship on which the vicomte had sailed had sunk one hour out of harbor, with the loss of all hands. The vicomte is thus disposed of fortuitously.

Dick returns to Paris and sadly relates these events to the vicomtesse. She is grieved, but she tells Dick that her marriage with the vicomte was really one of economic necessity. She had given up her real love many years ago. Meanwhile, Dick has faced Isabella with his grievances against her and has made it clear that he does not intend to marry her. She accepts this decision both bitterly and sadly. Turner has also told Lucille the true state of affairs in regard to Dick's fortune and his relationship to Isabella. This news, of course, changes Lucille's attitude toward Dick. Alphonse, too, has long since realized his mistake in suspecting Dick's motives and has given up his pursuit of Lucille because he realizes that even his regained fortune cannot buy her love. After Dick has finished consoling the vicomtesse about the defection of her husband, she sends him into the garden to Lucille, where the two young people come to an understanding.

It is learned that the Provence estates will support the vicomtesse comfortably and that Turner has written a new will, making Dick the heir to his fortune. This is a happy solution to Dick's future; the present can be handled easily by the serious-minded and responsible man who has developed from the happy-go-lucky Dick at the beginning of the story.

Merriman's attitude toward *Dross* gives some insight as to the soundness of his judgment as a critic of his own work. Perhaps he felt that he had sacrificed too much to plot and that many of his characters were more akin to pawns than to real people. Fate, in fact, seems to be the real protagonist in this story, but it may be that the author intended to convey precisely that impression. Dick Howard is fully realized, chiefly because he is permitted to develop all his latent abilities, once he has achieved a purpose in life. Madame De Clericy also emerges as a real person because of her deep sympathy and understanding and her ability to accept whatever life has to offer. She puts into words the author's implied criticism of marriages arranged on the basis of economic status when she says, referring to her own marriage with the vicomte, "I have an aim in existence which is in itself a happiness—to make Lucille's life a happy one, to ensure her that which I have missed, and to avoid a mistake made by generation after generation of women—namely, to believe that love comes to us after marriage" (326).[58]

John Turner, who appears in other works by Merriman, is the character who seems to be the most completely alive. Rotund, shrewd, he serves, like Karl Steinmetz in *The Sowers*, as the worldly-wise man of experience—the confidant and adviser to the sometimes bewildered hero. Humorously cynical, Turner sees situations in their true perspective and occasionally becomes the mouthpiece for the author's satirical aphorisms. "A pretty woman," he warns Dick on one occasion, "is never clever—she is too wise" (32). Toward the end of the story, when Turner tells Dick that he is leaving his fortune to him, Turner explains this act by saying: "A man who could refuse to marry such a pretty girl as

Isabella Gayerson, with such an exceedingly pretty fortune as she possesses, deserves to have money troubles; so I bequeath 'em to you" (315).

Many of the other characters are rather flat, their exits and their entrances being dictated frequently by the exigencies of the plot. The vicomte is an interesting study, but the reader is not sufficiently prepared for his complete reversal at the end of the story. Little is said directly about Miste, who looms like an evil genius over the story; but his character is effectively revealed by the influence he has on those about him.

Merriman expresses his opinion very effectively on a variety of subjects, sometimes through one of his characters, sometimes in his own person as narrator. Dick Howard documents the author's apparent conviction that the English educational system was a pointless one when he says, "I received my education at Eton and at Cambridge University. If you want a secretary to bowl you a straight ball, or pull a fairly strong oar, I am your man, for I learnt little else. I possess, indeed, the ordinary education of an English gentleman, sufficient Latin to misread an epitaph or a motto, and too little Greek to do me any harm" (21–22).

Merriman's staunch support of the monarchy is generally expressed indirectly, as in this indictment of democracy: "Republicanism was indeed in the air at this time. And has not history demonstrated that those who cry loudest for a commonwealth are such as wish to draw from that wealth and add nothing to it? The reddest Republican is always the man who has nothing to lose and all to gain by a social upheaval" (86).

·There is not only undeniable humor, but a very timely and immediate quality for us in such satirical observations as the following: "It is indeed love that makes the world go round—love of money" (113). The world of the late nineteenth century is again brought very close to our own by this observation: "At all times the world has possessed an army of geniuses whose greatness consists of faith and not of works—of faith in themselves which takes the outward form of weird clothing, long hair, and a literary or artistic pose. Paris streets were so full of such in 1870 that all thoughtful men would scarce fail to recognize a nation in its decadence" (162).

Often *Dross* demonstrates the author's facility with language—

his ability to evoke a striking image with an aptly turned phrase, as when he says that "The Baron Giraud emerged from the satin-lined recesses of the dainty carriage like a stout caterpillar from a rose, a stumpy little man with no neck and a red face" (77). Impressive too are Merriman's descriptions of place, particularly when the place, as in the following excerpt, must have been one that he knew and loved. In such passages, he conveys to the reader, not only the illusion of absolute reality, but also the nostalgia which he himself had for the past:

Very different from this was the ancient chateau of La Pauline, perched half-way up the mountain on a table-land—its grey stone face showing grimly against a sombre background of cypress trees. The house was built, as the antiquarians of Draguignan avow, of stone that was hewn by the Romans for less peaceful purposes. That an ancient building must have stood here would, indeed, be to some extent credible, from the fact that in front of the house lies a lawn of that weedless turf which is only found in this country in such places as the Arena at Frejus. In the center of the lawn stands a sun dial—grey, green and ancient—a relic of those days when men lived by hours, and not by minutes, as we do today. It is all of the old world—of that old, old world of France beside which our British antiquities are, with a few exceptions, youthful. This was the birthplace of Madame De Clericy and of Lucille herself. Hither the ladies always returned with a quiet joy. There is no more peaceful spot on earth than La Pauline, chiefly, perhaps, because there is nothing in nature so still and lifeless as an olive grove. Why, by the way, do the birds of the air never build their nests in these trees—why do they rarely rest and never sing here? Behind La Pauline—so close, indeed, that the little chapel stands in the grey hush of the trees, guarded, of course, by a sentinel circle of cypresses—rise the olive terraces and stretch up, tier above tier, till the pines are reached. Below the grey house the valley opens out like a fan, and far away to the south the rugged crags of Roquebrune stand out against a faint blue haze, which is the Mediterranean (73–74).

This description also illustrates the author's skill in observation, for the scene is sketched with a painter's eye and with his ability to select just the right details for the purpose at hand. Nowhere else in his entire work does Merriman reveal more successfully his genuine and life-long affinity for the Mediterranean scene.

X The Isle of Unrest

Malcolm Elwin refers to *The Isle of Unrest,* which appeared both as a book and as a serial in *Cornhill* in 1900, as "probably the best English novel about Corsica." [59] Like *Dross,* this novel is also set against the background of the Franco-Prussian War, but the action, with the exception of a few scenes in Paris, takes place in Corsica, an untamed land that seems well chosen to display the frequent violence of the events.

Denise Lange, the daughter of a deceased French army officer and a teacher in a girls' school in Paris, learns that she has been willed the Corsican estate of her father's cousin, Mattei Perucca, who has recently died in Corsica. She is surprised to receive shortly afterwards an offer to buy her property from Colonel Louis Gilbert, the military governor of Corsica. Denise, however, determines to occupy her Corsican property. Her elderly friend and fellow teacher, Mlle. Brun, who had once been in love with Denise's father, decides to accompany her.

In Corsica, meanwhile, the agent of Mattei Perucca, Pietro Andrei, has been mysteriously shot. Colonel Gilbert sends a letter warning of the renewal of the code of the vendetta to Mattei Perucca, the owner of Casa Perucca. This so enrages Mattei that he dies of a heart attack. Later Colonel Gilbert meets Lory de Vasselot while visiting the Baron and Baroness Melide in Paris. He offers to buy Lory's Corsican estates, but Lory refuses to sell; the offer is made although he thinks the land worthless, having been taught to believe this by his dead mother who had left Corsica thirty years before, presumably at the death of Lory's father, the Count de Vasselot.

At the home of the Melides, Lory meets Denise, who is a friend of Jane Melide. Upon learning that Denise is going to Corsica, Lory advises against it, but he also advises her not to sell. Later Lory, who has fallen in love with Denise, announces that he too is going to Corsica. Arriving at his estate in Corsica, he finds his father living in the casa in hiding, his mentality having suffered during his thirty years' hermitage. The old count tells Lory that he lives thus because he shot Andrei Perucca, Mattei's brother, thirty years ago. It is learned later that he shot Andrei because he and

Lory's mother were suspected of being intimate. This is the real reason why the Countess de Vasselot had left Corsica.

Denise and Mlle. Brun arrive at Casa Perucca in Corsica and find that the widow of Pietro Andrei, the man who had been recently shot, is the housekeeper there. They find that they are unwelcome in Corsica, so far as the suspicious natives are concerned. Colonel Gilbert proposes marriage to Denise after again being rebuffed by Lory in an attempt to buy Lory's estate. Denise, by now in love with Lory, refuses Gilbert.

The Franco-Prussian War breaks out, and Lory goes to France to join his regiment. Colonel Gilbert learns of the existence of the old Count de Vasselot and intimates to Denise that Lory has had "someone" living in his chateau. This of course has the desired effect of making her jealous and disinclined to trust Lory. The book then traces the course of the Franco-Prussian War to the defeat at Sedan and the consequent loss of the war. Lory plays a heroic part, as does Baron Melide, who establishes a hospital at the front.

The Abbé Susini undertakes to look out for Denise and Mlle. Brun. He also knows the secret regarding the old Count de Vasselot, and he eventually persuades Denise and Mlle. Brun to leave Corsica because of what may happen there as a result of the war. He plans to persuade the old count to leave, but finds him already gone. The party is to be taken from Corsica in Melide's yacht, arrangements having been made by Lory and the baron through the abbé. Mlle. Brun decides to join Baron Melide, to help him with his field hospital. The abbé instructs her to find Lory and tell him that the old count, his father, has disappeared. She does eventually find Lory in the hospital and gives him the news about his father and Denise. Later, she takes Lory back to Melide's estate at Frejus to recuperate from a wound. There Lory finds Denise again, but she is quite cool to him.

A traveler from Corsica tells Lory that his chateau has been burned to the ground. Lory, who wants to locate his father, discloses to Denise that he is going back to Corsica. She tries to dissuade him, but to no avail; and she and Mlle. Brun also decide to return to Corsica. There Denise agrees to sell Casa Perucca to Colonel Gilbert. They are delayed from signing the papers by

Mlle. Brun who has accidentally discovered gold on the land of the two estates and now understands why Gilbert is so desirous of acquiring Casa Perucca. She does not, however, reveal this knowledge. A hearing before a notary is arranged for the title transfer, and Mlle. Brun enlists the aid of the abbé in bringing Lory to help her to forestall Gilbert.

Having arrived in Corsica, Lory seeks his father in the mountain camps of the outlaws. He finds him at last, but the count does not recognize his son and tries to escape. Lory fires into the air to stop his father's horse. The horse shies, throws the old man, and kills him. The deeds to both de Vasselot's estate and Casa Perucca are found on Count de Vasselot's body. It appears that he really owned both estates; hence Perucca is not Denise's to sell.

At the hearing, the abbé reveals all the threads of the plot. Gilbert knew of the gold and arranged to revive the feud between the adherents of de Vasselot and those of Perucca by having Perucca's agent shot. He then tried by various ways to gain the estates, finally burning down de Vasselot's chateau in the hope of destroying the deeds. The colonel does not deny the charges, but he leaves to rejoin the army in a new attempt to drive back the Germans. Lory also rejoins the army, despite Denise's urging to the contrary. He and Gilbert meet during an attack; in the very same attack Gilbert is killed, and Lory is wounded beside him. During Lory's second convalescence at the Melides', all the misunderstandings between him and Denise are cleared away.

The Isle of Unrest presents yet another study of an essentially likeable character, Colonel Gilbert, who is ruined by selfishness and greed. The story emphasizes not only the effects of his acts on Gilbert himself but also the far-reaching consequences of his self-interest upon a number of innocent persons with whom he becomes associated. Of secondary interest is the theme which demonstrates the power of love to dissipate a longstanding feud.

When materialism comes into conflict with Merriman's basic idealism, as it does in this story, he usually delivers some penetrating observations on human nature and on the socio-economic conditions of his time. This book is a case in point. The rising middle class he characterizes on one occasion as "the new nobility, which is based, as all the world knows, on solid manufacture" (41).[60] He deprecates self-interest by implication when he says that "there are certain warm hearts that are happy in always loving, not the highest, but the nearest" (59). Concerning the growing gulf between poverty and affluence, he observes ironically: "Even the very poor may be charitable; they can think kindly of the rich" (231). Of those who proceed without purpose in life, he says, "The majority of people spoil their lives by going out to meet the future, deliberately converting into a reality that which was only dread" (244). His impatience with the heedlessness of the basically stupid is focused sharply in such comments as, "Intelligence betrays itself in listening more than in talking" (62); and "the dull or idle of intellect assuredly resemble each other in the patience with which they will listen to or tell the same story over and over again" (124).

An interesting contrast appears in the critical attitude to this book in the English and in the American *Bookman*. The English journal[61] finds nothing praiseworthy in the book except the title, which is descriptive of Corsica. The style is called "cynical and mannered," and the author is blamed for writing a "confused" plot and for monotonously flattering French women. Rather oddly, in a book about Corsica which is filled with descriptions of that island, the reviewer finds the descriptions "good but not germane." The American *Bookman*[62] comments on the "remarkable enthusiasm in the writing and expression of the spirit of Corsica," but it finds that the book is somewhat lacking in continuity and purpose, although the incidents and impressions are "vivid" and "excellent in themselves."

The *Athenaeum*[63] does little more than comment on the familiarity of the theme of a love that transcends the difficulties imposed by hereditary vengeance, while the *Academy*[64] points out the author's lack of enthusiasm for Napoleon III and refers to many of the epigrams as "flashes from the Obvious."

XI The Velvet Glove

Both Malcolm Elwin and Oliver Edwards[65] place *The Velvet Glove*, published in 1901, among Merriman's best books. Since he returns in this novel to the background of the Spanish Carlist rebellion, it is certainly another example of a genre in which he was generally very successful—the historical romance.

The author is concerned primarily in this book with the dangers inherent in revolutionary attempts to upset the political status quo and in the evils unleashed by the Jesuit philosophical tenet, as interpreted by Merriman, that the ends justify the means. He finds again in the disruption occasioned by the Carlist rebellion an argument to support his championship of monarchy, and his conception of the Jesuit intrigue to steal a young girl's fortune in order to buy political favors from the Carlists is a sufficient argument against the doctrine of expediency. The techniques of espionage are touched upon through the brief introduction of Cartoner and Deulin, two secret agents, who also play prominent roles in his next book, *The Vultures*.

The action of *The Velvet Glove* takes place almost entirely at various places in Spain during that period of the Carlist rebellion when the followers of Don Carlos were being supported by the Catholic Church, more particularly by the Jesuits, who felt that this faction offered them more than the Royalists. The scenes at Saragossa, Pampeluna, and the estate of Torre Garda in the Pyrenees furnish a colorful background for the action and permit the author a varied canvas for his descriptive powers.

Francisco de Mogente is slain upon his return to Saragossa after an absence of fifteen years. The attack on him is observed by his friend, Ramon de Sarrion, a Royalist like Francisco. Ramon, however, does not recognize Francisco's assailants. Francisco lives long enough after he is attacked to leave his fortune to his daughter, Juanita, instead of to his son, Leon, who has joined the Jesuit order. Evasio Mon, still friendly to Ramon, is present when this last-minute will is made.

Mon thinks it possible to force the youthful Juanita to enter a convent and to deliver the fortune, of which she still knows nothing, to the Jesuits, who in turn plan to use the money to hire the mercenary forces of General Pacheco to fight for the Carlists against the Royalists. The Jesuits have already conspired with the Carlists for political favors. Juanita is a devout pupil in the convent school of the Sisters of the True Faith, of which Sor Teresa, formerly Dolores de Sarrion, is the Sister Superior. Since Mon was once the suitor for Dolores's hand, he hopes to enlist her aid in his scheme. He is abetted in this plot by Juanita's brother, Leon. When Ramon de Sarrion learns of Mon's purpose in getting the fortune to aid the Carlist and the Jesuit cause, he, being a Royalist and the one-time friend of de Mogente, enlists the aid of his son, Marcos, to defeat the plot. Sor Teresa, although she pretends to agree with Mon, is in reality on the side of de Sarrion; and she tries subtly to impress upon Juanita the undesirable features of becoming a nun.

The Carlists assassinate Marshal Prim who leads the Royalist cause for Amedeo of Savoy, Duke of Aosta, the Royalist candidate to the throne of Spain. This event makes it even more imperative for the Jesuits to find the means of hiring Pacheco in order to prevent him from selling his services to the Royalists.

Marcos makes secret contact with Juanita at the convent in Pampeluna. He confirms the fact that Mon is really seeking to force the young girl into the convent in order to get her fortune to foster the Carlist cause. He and his father determine that the way to prevent this is for Marcos to marry Juanita secretly, in a love-less union because of the girl's youth. The wedding is accomplished by removing the girl from a religious procession, marrying her before a bishop friend of the Sarrions, and returning her to the convent before she is missed. When Mon visits the convent to try to persuade Juanita to accept his plan, the de Sarrions tell him of the marriage; and eventually Juanita is taken to the de Sarrion estate at Torre Garda. There she is visited by Evasio Mon and told that Marcos had married her only to secure her fortune for the Royalist cause.

She decides to go back to the convent at Pampeluna and become a nun, for she has begun to love Marcos and she is deeply hurt at being used as a pawn. Marcos is injured by a fall from a horse, but he follows her to make sure of her safety, for a pitched battle is soon to take place between the remnants of the Carlists and the Royalist forces, now augmented by the hired mercenaries of General Pacheco.

Juanita, at the urging of Sor Teresa, decides to return to Torre Garda and to Marcos. The battle takes place in the mountain valley of the Pyrenees where Torre Garda is located. Marcos brings Juanita back through the battle lines. During this battle Evasio Mon is killed, and the Royalist forces emerge victorious.

Marcos stays on at Torre Garda to recuperate, while his father goes back to Saragossa. Cousin Peligros, the housekeeper at Torre Garda, goes back to her house; and Juanita, now emotionally mature, stays on as the mistress of Torre Garda. She discovers that Marcos truly loves her, and she is ready at last to return that love.

Because of the extremely involved nature of their activities and interrelationships, many of the characters in this book seem to be motivated exclusively by forces outside of, rather than within, themselves. The mysterious Evasio Mon, particularly, appears as a coldly calculating intriguer, incapable of even a spark of human feeling. A similar lack of sensitivity afflicts Leon de Mogente in his attitude toward his sister. It is difficult to believe that even so dedicated a person as he could be quite so heartless in pursuit of the Jesuitical purpose. The de Sarrions, on the other hand, are admirable examples of gentlemanliness; and the simple and trusting Juanita is one of the author's most appealing female character creations. The historical aspects of the story are handled factually and forcefully, and verisimilitude is obtained by the introduction of some actual historical personages such as the Duke of Aosta and General Pacheco.

Swift-moving and tightly constructed, the plot is carefully unified by the common bond of interest among the characters involved in its intricacies. In this, as in many other respects, the book is conceived and written in the author's very best style.

The political and moral involvement of the Jesuits in the Carlist rebellion was, in the author's mind, one of the most serious complications of that struggle. His denunciation of the self-interest that, in his opinion, ruled the activities of the Jesuit organization is clear, but fair. "The heart [of the Jesuit organization] has done the best work that missionaries have yet accomplished," he says. "The head has ruined half Europe" (127).[66] Defending his own religion, Ramon de Sarrion says, "The Church—our Church —has enemies. It has Bismarck, and the English; but it has no worse enemy than the Jesuits. For they play their own game" (266).

While Merriman's preference seems to be for an earlier and less complicated era, he frequently discloses his full cognizance of the shifting values of his own society. More often than not, his perception is accompanied by disapproval. Concerning woman's place on the social scale, Marcos de Sarrion is ironically reported to hold

. . . odd views—now deemed chivalrous and old-fashioned—on the
question of a woman's liberty to seek her own happiness in her own
way. Such views are unnecessary today when woman is, so to speak,
up and fighting. They belong to the days of our grandmothers, who
had less knowledge and much more wisdom; for they knew that it is
always more profitable to receive a gift than demand a right. The
measure will be fuller   (232).

Merriman's appreciation for the genuine over the spurious values in life is further emphasized by his observation that "There
are many in these days of cheap imitation of the medieval who
feel the same" (124); that it is possible to learn more from the
past than from the uneasy present.

In reviewing the book, the *Academy* records the fact that *The
Velvet Glove* is second only to the latest story by Anthony Hope
among the six most popular books of 1902.[67] While the reviewer is
pleased with the soundness of the plot and with the delineation of
the characters, except for Evasio Mon, he deprecates the "sententious, obvious, dull epigrams." The *Athenaeum*[68] also notes the
tendency to excessive moralizing, but finds the story good and the
attitude toward the Jesuits harsh but fair. The reviewer praises
the "fine dramatic instinct" of the scenes and asserts that "This
[book] will add to the author's reputation." The *Dial* compares
Merriman's book to the latest work of Stanley Weyman, *Count
Hannibal,* which is also a story of Carlist adventure in the 1870's.
"The Jesuit," continues this reviewer, "is Merriman's *bête noire*
and he paints a dark picture of Jesuitical intrigue in behalf of the
reactionary cause." [69] Like most of the other reviews, this one
praises the plot structure and the individuality of the characters,
but it objects to "a lack of finish" in certain details which "leaves
minor incidents without proper logical development."

XII   The Vultures

The Vultures, published in 1902, combines several of the author's major themes. Most prominent of these, perhaps, is the necessity for an unwavering sacrifice to duty, as this is exemplified
particularly in the persons of the British intelligence agent, Reginald Cartoner, and in the three Bukatys, as well as in the revolutionary, Kosmaroff. This book, too, presents a thorough exposition

of the methods of intelligence operatives—a theme which is less fully developed in a number of the author's other novels. In *The Vultures,* the problem is approached through the activities of Reginald Cartoner, a British agent; Paul Deulin, a French agent; and Joseph Mangles, a United States agent. In addition, there is considerable attention given to the activities of unofficial underground intelligence operatives, in the persons of Prince Bukaty and his son Martin. A third thematic interest is centered in the menace to the world's peace of the revolutionary movement represented by the ruthless Kosmaroff, and in the patent injustices of tyranny as it is exercised by the Russians in their cruel persecution of the helpless Poles. A minor but important theme of *The Vultures* is concerned with the author's conviction that injuries to the married state are engendered, unintentionally but inevitably, by the parties joined in the marriage, never by outside influences.

The drama of *The Vultures* is played principally in Warsaw and in Russia against the background of Poland's abortive struggle to free itself of Russian domination:

Less than forty years ago a crowd of Poles assembled in the square in front of the castle to protest against the tyranny of their conquerors. They were unarmed, and when the Russian soldiery fired upon them, they stood and cheered, and refused to disperse. Again, in cold blood, the troops fired, and the Warsaw massacre continued for three hours in the streets   (67).[70]

At the opening of the story, three men whose presence in a given area usually signifies trouble are on their way to Warsaw. They have been ordered there by their respective governments to ferret out any available information about a suspected uprising of the Poles against their Russian conquerors. Reginald Cartoner, a British secret agent, is dedicated to the job which he performs with machine-like precision and accuracy. Paul Deulin, a French agent, is sophisticated and debonair, but equally efficient. The middle-aged American agent, Joseph P. Mangles, is traveling with his niece, the shallow but kindly Netty Cahere, and his sister, Julia Mangles, a comical spinster and militant feminist who dissipates her energies in pointless charities and in battling for a multitude of lost causes. Despite his native shrewdness, Mangles is regarded rather patronizingly by Cartoner and Deulin. As Deulin himself says, "If he had been properly trained, he might have done something, that Joseph P. Mangles; for he can hold his tongue. But he took to it late, as they all do in America" (36). These three men are often referred to, in a grimly humorous vein, as the "vultures" because their foregathering indicates the imminence of serious trouble.

The secret agents, particularly Cartoner, are friends of the Bukaty family, composed of Prince Bukaty, his son Martin, and his daughter Wanda. The Bukatys are intensely patriotic Poles, who, having been dispossessed of their great estates by the Russians, are now working with the Polish revolutionaries—led by a former nobleman, Kosmaroff—to help Poland regain her place as a nation. Specifically, they are currently engaged in arranging, through Captain Cable, for shipments of arms to be delivered to the Poles in preparation for the projected uprising which is to synchronize with the attempted assassination of the czar of Russia.

Although Cartoner and Wanda fall in love virtually at first sight, both decide to postpone plans for marriage until he is no longer bound by duty as an intelligence agent and until she, as a true patriot, has performed her duty to her family and to her country. Both of them realize that they must avoid each other for the present so that Cartoner's position will not be compromised and so that no suspicion of defection on the part of the Bukatys will be aroused in the mind of Kosmaroff, who, in his violent way, is also in love with Wanda.

Netty Cahere is fascinated by the glamor attaching to Martin Bukaty as the potential champion of his downtrodden country and fancies herself in love with him. Although she is slow to realize it, Netty is really in love with Cartoner. Martin, on the other hand, sincerely loves Netty.

By amassing bits of evidence Cartoner discovers the hiding place of the smuggled armory and narrowly escapes death at the hands of Kosmaroff, who is restrained from his intention by Martin Bukaty. Eventually the Polish revolt proves abortive, and Martin is killed by a stray bullet while attempting to escape by boat. Netty, apparently unaffected by his death, eventually marries a wealthy promoter. Still placing duty above personal desire, Wanda feels that she must comfort her father, who, broken by the failure of the Polish bid for freedom, has gone into hiding. Although the "vultures" can now relax their watchfulness for a while, Cartoner will of course wait for Wanda, as she has waited for him.

Aside from the natural excitement which this story arouses because of its exposition of espionage activities, the book is an interesting study in plot structure. All the elements of the story seem to mesh perfectly with the main theme. The various subplots concerned with the activities of the well-intentioned Mangles and his busybody sister "Jooly," the romantic entanglements of the flirtatious Netty Cahere, and the attempts to check the bloodthirsty inclinations of Kosmaroff are well unified; and they help to develop and strengthen the main plot instead of diverting attention from it. The characters, too, are clearly defined and multidimensional, especially Joseph and Julia Mangles, Paul Deulin, Cartoner, and Wanda Bukaty. Even Karl Steinmetz, who makes a brief appearance as a sort of unofficial observer of international complications, is entirely consistent with the detailed portrait drawn of him in *The Sowers*.

There are echoes of both Dickens and Thackeray in this book. The opportunistic Netty Cahere has more than a hint of Becky Sharp, and Joseph Mangles and his sister are in the Dickensian tradition, although Merriman treats his Americans much more gently than Dickens did. On one occasion the author makes direct reference to Thackeray when he allows Deulin to describe himself as " 'only a little stall in Vanity Fair, with everything displayed to the best advantage in the sunshine' " (155).

Merriman's handling of the historical background is impressively convincing, and his visualization of the Warsaw scene is an outstanding addition to his extensive gallery of entirely credible places. This is particularly true in passages where he contrasts the brilliance of Warsaw as the capital of an independent nation with its bleakness under Russian domination.

The book offers many examples of the author's favorite narrative techniques. Suspense through foreshadowing is built by such confidences as "by nine o'clock that work was begun which was to throw a noose round the necks of Prince Bukaty, Prince Martin, Captain Petersen, and several others" (27). Merriman looks realistically at intelligence work when he causes Deulin to say of

Mangles, " 'He is in the service of his country, my friend, like any other poor devil . . . He spends half his time kicking his heels in New York, or wherever they kick their heels in America. The rest of his time he is risking his health, or possibly his neck, wherever it may please the fates to send him' " (36).

Merriman's social and political philosophy is reiterated in occasional asides. His usual disillusion with the purposelessness of much social activity is reflected in "It was also dimly perceptible that there was a larger proportion of brain in the room than is allotted to the merely fashionable, or to that shallow mixture of the dramatic and pictorial, which usually designated the artistic world." Or: "From living much alone he had acquired the habit of wondering whether it was worth while to say that which came into his mind—which is a habit fatal to social success" (37, 42). Distrust of the democratic process is echoed in "It is the odor of Monarchy, slowly fading from the face of a world that reeks of cheap democracy" (87). In opposition to the democratic ideal of acting as one's brother's keeper, Merriman preferred the *laissez-faireism* implicit in contemplating "our neighbor's life with that calm indifference to his good or ill which is the only true philosophy" because "the gods amuse themselves with men as children amuse themselves with toys" (138). Concerning the relationship between the sexes, the author asserts that "half the trouble of this troubled world comes from the fact that, for one reason or another, women are not always able to look up to the men with whom they have dealings" (142).

Part of the appeal of this book for a reader today would surely be the timeliness engendered by the dramatic parallel that can be drawn between the situation in the story and that in the world about us. This may result from sheer accident, but it may also be valid to assume that in *The Vultures*—and in certain other books such as *With Edged Tools, The Sowers, Flotsam,* and *Roden's Corner*—the author wisely chose themes which have the quality of universality. Merriman's prophetic foreshadowing of the Russian menace to the world is made explicit in Martin Bukaty's description of his own people: " '. . . we Poles are under a cloud in Europe now. We are the wounded man by the side of the road from Jerusalem down to Jericho, and there is a tendency to pass by on the other side. We are a nation with a bad want, and it is nobody's business to satisfy it. Everybody is ready, however, to admit that we have been confoundedly badly treated'" (62). Merriman wrote in 1902 there is "a sinister sound in the very name of Russia" (269).

The *Athenaeum* calls this story of Poland one of the author's best, quietly and competently written "with excellent feeling for the Polish struggles." [71] It notes especially the worldly wisdom in the book and the effective handling of the struggles of both the Russian Nihilists and the determined Poles to overthrow their oppressors.

The *Academy* finds Merriman's places much more vivid than his history, but, this notice continues, whether historically true or not, the book "reads convincingly." [72] Many of the reflections and asides are referred to as platitudinous, and the ever-dependable Cartoner is singled out as "Merriman's ideal character."

The American *Bookman* states that *The Vultures* is full of "robust, imaginative writing" possessed of "easy strength and charm." The author is particularly praised for his descriptions, both of persons and places, which "stand out like etchings." [73]

XIII Barlasch of the Guard

Oliver Edwards is of the opinion that *"Barlasch of the Guard* has been in England his [Merriman's] most widely read and best-loved story." [74] Apparently, the British Broadcasting Corporation would concur in this judgment, for it once broadcast *Barlasch* in serial form.[75]

Published in 1903, the year of Merriman's death, *Barlasch of the Guard,* like *The Vultures,* explores a number of related themes. Prominent among these is a consideration of the waste and futility of war, especially in terms of the resulting human suffering. This suffering extends not only to the conquered peoples of Dantzig, but also to their Napoleonic conquerors and even to the Russians who eventually succeed in turning back Napoleon's decimated legions. Equally important is the exposition given to the activities of military secret service and espionage. Charles Darragon, who marries Désirée Sebastian, and Colonel de Casimir are members of Napoleon's secret service and are chiefly concerned with spying out plots against Napoleon's life. Louis d'Arragon, Charles's cousin, is a British agent charged with keeping lines of communication open between Britain and Russia. Antoine Sebastian, father of Désirée and Mathilde, is suspected of being a former French aristocrat; he is now a member of the Tugendbund, a secret organization working democratically for a free Dantzig and pledged to unalterable opposition toward Napoleon. Between the warmongers and those who seek to liquidate them stands Sergeant Barlasch, a sort of untutored Humanist, whose loyalties are firmly pledged to those he loves, and one whose political sympathies, like those of the author, might be summed up in the phrase "a plague o' both your houses." Through his frequent castigation of the thinkers and talkers who foment discord and war, Merriman makes it perfectly clear that his own preference is for those who, like Barlasch and Louis d'Arragon, discharge their duty with justice and humanity, always eschewing the selfish motive.

Most of the story takes place in Dantzig in 1812, just before, during, and after Napoleon's unsuccessful Russian campaign. There are some especially graphic descriptions of certain phases of the battles at Vilna, Kowno, and Borodino; in fact, the author's handling of the events at Borodino might be favorably compared to Tolstoy's treatment of that battle.

Antoine Sebastian, whose possible aristocratic past as a French nobleman is never divulged by the author, is a teacher of the violin and the conductor of a dance studio in Dantzig. His daughters, Désirée and Mathilde, are teachers in the school. The real reason for Antoine's presence in Dantzig is to direct the activities of the Tugendbund.

At the opening of the story, Désirée has just married a young officer in Napoleon's army, Charles Darragon, and she is unaware that he has been stationed in Dantzig by Napoleon to spy on the Tugendbund. Also present in Dantzig are Louis d'Arragon, who has been sent there by England as an intelligence observer, and Colonel de Casimir, associated with Charles in the French secret service. It was de Casimir who introduced Charles to Désirée at a reception at the home of General Rapp, the military protector stationed in Dantzig by Napoleon. Désirée's elder sister, Mathilde, has fallen in love with the fascinating and mysterious de Casimir.

Napoleon's army moves into Dantzig in preparation for the projected Russian campaign, and with it comes Sergeant "Papa" Barlasch, an old trooper of Napoleon's army who is quartered with the Sebastians. Although the Sebastians are opposed to Napoleon, Barlasch attaches himself to the family and makes himself Désirée's unofficial protector.

Shortly after his marriage, Charles is called to the front and there reports to his superior, Colonel de Casimir, on the activities of his father-in-law, Antoine. Charles writes a report in which he asserts that Antoine is the one member of the Tugendbund to be feared; if an attempt were to be made on Napoleon's life in Dantzig, Antoine would be the one to make it. Charles returns home briefly before joining his regiment, bringing with him his cousin, Louis d'Arragon, whom Désirée thus meets for the first time. She is immediately attracted by Louis's quiet strength. Louis himself, of course, does not explain that he is really in Dantzig as an English agent whose duty is to keep lines of communication open between England and Russia.

Mathilde makes clear her love for de Casimir, who has temporarily been left behind in Dantzig. She loves him for his strength, ambition, and ruthlessness, and partly out of spite because she, the elder sister, is not yet married. De Casimir seeks Mathilde's help in keeping informed about the Tugendbund. He promises that he will protect her father.

Barlasch, in his role of protector, warns Désirée of activity against the Tugendbund and intimates that he has heard that Sebastian is in reality a French nobleman who had escaped the guillotine. This impression is strengthened because, from his manner, Sebastian appears to have known Louis d'Arragon's father, who also escaped the guillotine by fleeing to England. However, this point about Sebastian's identity is not cleared up in the story. Barlasch takes Sebastian's place in the latter's room when the constabulary come to arrest Sebastian, who is hidden elsewhere. At Barlasch's urging, Désirée goes to Louis to get him to help her father escape on the ship with which Louis has been furnished in order to get messages back and forth from England to Russia.

Mathilde thinks de Casimir responsible for her father's disappearance and goes to question him. He convinces her that this is not the case and tells her it was Désirée who managed the escape. It is then that she reveals her love for him.

Later Barlasch volunteers to arrange for Sebastian's return from exile, now that the war has moved on from Dantzig. Accordingly, he instructs Louis, who brings Sebastian back.

A brief account is given of the pursuit by the French of the wily Russian general, Kutusoff, who withdraws to Borodino, within sight of Moscow, where the French army, being without supplies or reserves, is decimated. In the battle, Charles loses some papers which are returned to Désirée by the military authorities who believe that Charles is dead. From them she learns of his part in betraying her father. A note accompanies the papers, assuring her that Charles was seen alive after the battle. She informs Louis of Charles's activities as a spy.

Barlasch encounters Charles and de Casimir in Moscow and Charles gives him a letter to deliver to Désirée, not knowing who he really is. Barlasch returns to Dantzig bringing news of Charles and the battle, and of Napoleon's one-night sojourn in Moscow. Napoleon returns to Paris.

News that General Rapp is to occupy Dantzig for Napoleon causes Désirée to wish to get her father out of Dantzig again. She sends Barlasch with a message for Louis, and he and Barlasch go out in search of Charles. Barlasch returns with the news that de Casimir and Charles are safe in Vilna. Barlasch then conducts Désirée to Louis, who in turn will take her to Charles. They find de Casimir ill, traveling under Charles's name. He, thinking that Charles has gone to Dantzig, says they changed identities because Charles was to take two carriages full of captured Russian treasures to Paris, but he wished to go to Dantzig instead. De Casimir, who wanted to go to Paris anyhow, changed identities with him and took charge of the treasure.

Mathilde leaves to join de Casimir in Cracow, in response to a message he had sent by Louis. Barlasch undertakes to take care of Désirée and Sebastian during the Russian siege of Dantzig, now under the command of General Rapp whom the Dantzigers hate.

Louis finally finds the body of Charles at St. Basile's Hospital in Vilna. Meanwhile, Sebastian has died of the rigors of the siege. Upon returning to Dantzig, Barlasch reveals that de Casimir, when they met him at Vilna, already knew that Charles was dead. He implies that de Casimir bought his amnesty with the Russian treasure. Louis sends for Désirée and she goes through the siege lines, under Barlasch's guidance, to join Louis. Barlasch, seeking to draw attention from Désirée, is shot and killed; but Désirée and Louis are united at last.

From the standpoints of structure and characterization, *Barlasch* ranks very high in the roster of Merriman's novels. The incidents of the plot are dramatic in themselves, and there is a natural cohesiveness from scene to scene which causes one situation to lead smoothly to another. The dramatic impact of the story is particularly impressive in the accounts of Napoleon's Russian campaign, which are narrated with considerable fidelity to realistic detail. The human relationships are handled with great restraint; sometimes more is conveyed by what is left unsaid than by what is said.

While most of the characters are successfully and carefully differentiated, Barlasch himself is the most vivid and convincing one in the book. Naïvely and humorously humanitarian, Barlasch is the catalyst that quickens the illusion of reality. His basic nature, moreover, is consistently maintained to the very end, and his sacrificial death is a fitting climax to his life-long unselfishness. The man of action, Louis d'Arragon, is cast in the same heroic mold as Theodore Trist, Prince Paul, and Reginald Cartoner; and Désirée, although somewhat lacking in warmth, admirably fulfills the requirements for a Merriman heroine.

Many of the author's philosophical asides are somewhat cynical, but discerning. Concerning the era of which he was writing, he says: "This was not an age in which the individual life was highly valued. Men were great today and gone tomorrow. Women were of small account. It was the day of deeds and not of words. In these latter times all that is changed, and the talker has a hearing" (53).[76] In a similar vein, he again champions the doers as opposed to the thinkers and talkers when he observes that "Someday the world will learn to have a greater respect for the workers than for the thinkers, who are idle, wordy persons, frequently thinking wrong" (52).

His feminine ideal of perfection can be pieced together partially from such comments as the following:

There are some maidens who require no better chaperone for their hearts than their own heads.

. . . .

Experience in a woman is tantamount to a previous conviction against a prisoner.

. . . .

. . . some men are honest and unselfish, all their lives, which perhaps means that they remain in love—for the first time—all their lives. They are rare, of course. But the sort of woman with whom it is possible to remain in love all through a life-time is rarer   (38, 42).

Naturally, this novel offers a number of observations on war and its aftermath. In the quotations that follow, Merriman clearly indicates that he is not deluded by any romantic attitudinizing in this respect. "It is only in war," he says wryly, "that the unexpected admittedly happens. In love and other domestic calamities there is always a relative who knew it all the time" (123). In another instance, he calls war "the gambling of kings" (135); and again "war either hardens or softens. It never leaves a man as it found him" (328). We have always had ample evidence of the uncertainty of military alliances. Merriman voiced this uncertainty forcefully in referring to the fact that "some who were allies today were commanded by their kings to slay each other tomorrow" (46). But his bitterest indictment occurs in his allusion to the division of the spoils of conquest when, inevitably, "the poor in all the lands rather naturally conclude that God will think of carriage people first" (226).

The reviewer for the English *Bookman*[77] claimed for the novel "pathos and humor, with ease and vividness of style," but the author was chastised for marring the book with cynical epigrams and aphorisms and for the "fretful affectation" displayed in his "gibes at men and women . . . better left to smaller men." Barlasch was called a "quaintly humorous and human figure" finely drawn and well contrasted with the other characters.

Noting that the book was, during most of 1903, appearing as a serial in the *Cornhill* magazine, the *Athenaeum*[78] objected to this somewhat non-romantic work by a romanticist. The use of history is praised, as are the characterizations and the restraint of the writing, but the moralizing is deprecated and the story is said to "lack blood" and the ability to "quicken the reader's pulse."

The novelist's sense of form and brisk movement is singled out for commendation by the reviewer for the *Academy*.[79] The originality and effectiveness of the author's "sarcastic sentiments" are also pointed out. The war segments of the story are characterized as "graphic," and the book is compared to Erckmann-Chatrian's *Le Blocus* because of the Napoleonic theme, the latter work being called superior to *Barlasch* in the portrayal of military characters.

XIV The Last Hope

Merriman's final novel, *The Last Hope,* was published posthumously in 1904. The story is concerned in part with the putative career of the "lost Dauphin," who, according to legend, escaped the fate of his father, Louis XVI, during the French Revolution. Principally, however, this is the story, not of Louis's son, but of his hypothetical grandson. For the sake of his narrative, the author supposes that the Dauphin was brought as a child to the fishing village of Farlingford in England. There, his origins unknown, he grew to manhood as a simple fisherman referred to by his associates as "the Frenchman." There too he eventually married and had a son who was called Loo Barebone, an obvious corruption of a name which becomes, to those who later seek to regain for him the throne of France, one of the evidences of the young man's royal origin.

The attempt to restore Barebone to the French throne is foredoomed to failure because of the opportunistic attitude of most of those who promote the scheme. Loo himself first believes that he is unselfishly sacrificing personal desires to the call of destiny and duty. Gradually, however, he becomes convinced, through some chicanery of Dormer Colville's, that he is not really the grandson of Louis; but by this time he has become so enamored of the material possibilities of the situation that he persuades himself that he must go through with the plot for the ultimate good of France.

Dormer Colville is an English adventurer who believes that the end justifies the means. His interest as a promoter of Barebone's cause is strictly material. Although he is loyal to his fellow conspirators, he unscrupulously substitutes a picture of Marie Antoinette for that of another royal lady in a locket which Barebone has had since infancy. It is Barebone's discovery of this substitution that convinces him that he is not the rightful claimant to the throne.

The Marquis de Gemosac is the leader of the French Royalist group that seeks to restore the monarchy. Genuinely believing in the authenticity of Barebone's right to the throne, he traces Barebone with the help of Captain Clubbe, the forthright and honorable captain of "The Last Hope," a symbolically named ship which the Royalist conspirators have chartered for passages between England and France. Barebone is mate aboard this ship, and Captain Clubbe learns of the mysterious way in which Barebone's father, the Frenchman, had lived and died in Farlingford, and of the locket which the Frenchman had passed on to his son. The excitable, ineffectual Marquis is one of the few characters not motivated by self-interest.

John Turner, the English banker who operates in Paris, plays an important role in this story. His efforts to circumvent the Royalist plotters are dictated primarily by fear of resulting economic ruin to financial institutions like his own. Although he plots to have Barebone kidnapped and pretends bankruptcy for a time to prevent the Royalist sympathizer, Mrs. St. Pierre Lawrence, from withdrawing a large sum of money from his bank to contribute to the Royalist cause, he is deeply sympathetic toward Miriam Liston, the Farlingford rector's niece who, although she truly loves Loo, rejects him because she does not want to interfere in his high destiny. Even in her quiet grief at Barebone's eventual drowning, Miriam symbolizes the serenity of a life devoted completely and idealistically to the code of duty.

Thus Merriman uses this story of an abortive attempt to seize the French throne in the name of the "lost Dauphin" to underscore yet again the lesson that is implicit in almost everything he ever wrote—life is good only if it has purpose, and this purpose must be a worthy one; it must not be tainted with self-interest, opportunism, or materialism. At the end of the story, only Miriam and Captain Clubbe, both of whom have lived "four-square" in the captain's words, emerge virtually unscathed by the violent and greed-inspired events of the narrative. They are sustained by the inward knowledge that they have done consistently, not always perhaps what was right, for no one is omniscient, but always what they thought was right. This is the duty that man owes to himself and to society.

Miriam Liston's final action in *The Last Hope* epitomizes this philosophy, for the author says of her as she gazes upon the drowned body of her erstwhile lover, Barebone: "She looked down at him with tired eyes. She had done the right, and this was the end. There are some who may say that she had done what she thought was right, and this only seemed to be the end. It may be so" (442).[80]

Pared of these thematic complexities, the plot outline is simple enough. The Marquis de Gemosac and Dormer Colville seek out Loo Barebone, believing him to be the grandson of Louis XVI, and hence the legitimate claimant to the throne of France. They act for the Royalist party, consisting of Mrs. St. Pierre Lawrence, the de Chantonnays and others who are opposed to the politics of Louis Bonaparte, the Prince President of the French Republic. They believe the restoration of the monarchy to be the "last hope" of France.

These people convince Barebone that he is entitled to the throne. He goes to France and is accepted by nearly all those interested in the Royalist cause. The Marquis de Gemosac even encourages Barebone's interest in his daughter Juliette, but she rejects Barebone because she senses that he is really in love with someone else. Although the conspirators try to arrange it, Barebone is not permitted to visit the Duchesse d'Angoulême, the daughter of Marie Antoinette who still lives at Frohsdorf.

It begins to look as if the Royalists may be successful until John Turner, the banker, stops their funds. Then Louis Bonaparte saves his own political situation by seizing control of the government, and by making himself emperor in spite of the republican constitution. He then begins to hunt out the Royalist plotters. Albert de Chantonnay is imprisoned, De Gemosac, Dormer Colville, and Loo Barebone escape from France in "The Last Hope," but the ship is wrecked near Farlingford. Although the others are saved, Loo is drowned and washed ashore, to return in death to those who knew and loved him as a simple villager. Of all those who had once courted Barebone's favor, only de Gemosac continues to be convinced that he really was the grandson of Louis XVI.

Merriman's adept handling of the village scene and the sturdily independent village characters provides an interesting foil for his equally skillful portrayal of the luxurious Parisian environment of the Royalist sympathizers. His love of the sea and his early association with his father's merchant ships are revealed in numerous passages which, like the following, demonstrate his familiarity with his subject matter and his facility:

It was nearly the top of the tide and the clear green water swelled and gurgled round the weedy piles of the quay, bringing on its surface tokens from the sea—shadowy jelly-fish, weed, and froth. "The Last Hope" was quite close at hand now, swinging up in mid-stream. The sun had set and over the marshes the quiet of evening brooded lazily, Captain Clubbe had taken in all sail except a jib. His anchor was swinging lazily overside, ready to drop. The watchers on the Quay could note the gentle rise and fall of the crack little vessel as the tide lifted her from behind. She seemed to be dancing to her home like a maiden back from school. The swing of her tapering masts spoke of the heaving seas she had left behind.   (17)

The idyllic nature of the foregoing passage is in sharp contrast to the biting irony of the author's depiction of the brittle world of fashion, an example of the fact that his art could encompass both high and low degree:

It was, in fact, Madame de Chantonnay's Thursday evening to which were bidden such friends as enjoyed for the moment her fickle good graces. The Abbé Touvent was, so to speak, a permanent subscriber to these favours. The task was easy enough, and any endowed with a patience to listen, a readiness to admire that excellent young noble-man, Albert de Chantonnay, and the credulity necessary to listen to the record (more hinted at than clearly spoken) of Madame's own charms in her youth, could make sure of a game of dominoes on the evening of the third Thursday in the month   (336–37).

Just as are the two social levels themselves, so are the characters on each of these social levels sharply differentiated. The villagers of Farlingford are treated with the gentleness and respect shown by Hardy toward his Woodlanders. The de Chantonnays, the St. Pierre Lawrences, and the French world of fashion generally are mercilessly reflected in the mirror of their own shallow vanity. Merriman reinforces this judgment of the French upper class when he refers to "the best man that France has latterly pro-duced, and, so far as the student of racial degeneration may fore-tell, will ever produce again—her middle class woman" (132).

The Last Hope is, to some extent, an attack on the doctrine of political expediency and on the power for evil of rampant materialism. Dormer Colville voices the doctrine of political opportunism so detestable to Merriman: ". . . in politics it often turns out that a man's duty is to break his word—duty toward his party, and his country, and that sort of thing" (326). The author deplores in his own person the materialistic orientation of society which he has observed in his own time:

The wildest dreamer of those days never anticipated that, in the passage of one brief generation, social advancement should be for the shrewdly ignorant rather than for the scholar; that it would be better for a man that his mind be stored with knowledge of the world than the wisdom of the classics; that the successful grocer might find a kinder welcome in a palace than the scholar; that the manufacturer of kitchen utensils might feed with kings and speak to them, without aspirates, between the courses   (279–80).

It is of this world that he observes ironically, ". . . friendship may perish from some other cause—a marriage, or success in life, one of the two great severers" (97).

The reviews of this book were generally quite favorable. It is possible, of course, that the reviewers may have been thus impelled by respect for a man recently deceased, but the objectivity of most of the notices does not bear this out. The English *Bookman*[81] comments on the fact that the story is told with great restraint, without under-plot, and with moralizing left to the reader. These techniques, the review continues, are French, like the story itself. While the handling of the story is thus reminiscent of Racine, its color is modern and romantic. The central problem of the way in which the grown son of the supposedly escaped Dauphin would face the world is, in the opinion of the reviewer, one that Browning might play with. Although the characters are well drawn, they are somewhat lacking in depth; and the book, because of the theatricality of its scenes, is likened to "a libretto, hardly expanded, with definite scenes, but not . . . that suggestion of a walk through life which it is the novelist's duty and privilege to convey."

The *Academy*[82] speaks of the professional manner in which the story is told and of the assurance and definiteness of the style.

This smoothness, however, is, in the reviewer's opinion, "marred by habitual would-be epigrams." The portrait of the banker, John Turner, is found to be one of the "most convincing character sketches" in the book.

XV *Realism and Romance Combined*

Between 1892 and 1904 Merriman wrote fourteen novels, all but one of which would probably be considered by the author himself as his major work. Since it was his decision to withdraw from publication the four books appearing prior to 1892 and *Dross* in 1899, it seems reasonable to assume that he was quite willing to be represented by the thirteen remaining novels. Although he professed to be opposed to the growing vogue for Realism, in these books he was able to adapt, with considerable success, the techniques of Realism to the popular romance, an achievement which places him among the transitional figures in respect to the literary practices of his time.

The themes which constantly recur in these novels show a developing awareness of man's obligations to himself and to his environment. Merriman speaks eloquently of the necessity of living according to a preconceived purpose and an awareness of the overriding importance of duty. He seizes every opportunity to point out the destructive effects, both individually and collectively, of self-interest and opportunism. Basically an idealist, he believed that good must eventually triumph over evil; but he was fully cognizant of the evil potential of a rampant materialism. His favorite hero was the gentleman adventurer who, in the guise of empire builder, intelligence agent, war correspondent, humanitarian, or soldier of fortune did his conscientious best to right the world's wrongs. For the vacillations of those who think or talk a situation to death, Merriman had nothing but contempt. His heroines were loyal, patient, composed, and constant; but, when occasion offered, they could be ardent as well. Whether male or female, the villains were moved to their unorthodox practices by some innate tragic fault that caused them to succumb to temptation beyond their strength.

Temperamentally, Merriman was opposed to the taint of professionalism in matters of reform. He conceived of charity in the Biblical sense, always seeking the selfish motive behind the "do-gooder." He believed, furthermore, that ruthless acts by such religious and racial groups as the Jesuits and the Jews were dictated by the convenient expediency of any means to an end.

On the social and political levels, he recognized philosophically the tremendous problem posed by the downtrodden masses victimized by social and political tyranny. His remedy, however, was evolution rather than revolution, for he realized fully the corrosive effect on society of hatred and warfare. All of this resulted in a humanitarian and conservatively democratic political philosophy within the framework of that government by benevolent monarchy which he most admired.

With few exceptions, Merriman's novels demonstrated increasing evidence of the author's control over his material. His plot structure became more cohesive, with less emphasis on the subplot. Despite this careful structural tailoring, his less successful books sometimes conveyed the impression that the plot was manipulated for effect rather than allowed to grow naturally out of character. Although the earlier books had individual scenes which were highly dramatic but somewhat disconnected, the later volumes tended to develop a more cumulative dramatic impact, along with a more penetrating observation of places and people. The author's economy of narration also became more marked, to the point where he was able to convey as much by what he left unsaid as by what he said. In some of his earlier work there was a noticeable tendency to leave unresolved certain minor situations in the story, but his later work showed a conscientiousness in drawing together these narrative threads, as well as a deft assurance in the timing of the denouement and in the use of figurative language. Perhaps few writers, moreover, have been able to convey to a reader more successfully the best qualities of ladies and gentlemen. Such portraits are seldom overdrawn, but are presented with such clarity, honesty, and vigor as to excite the reader's genuine admiration. Equally impressive, though certainly not admirable, are many of those fictional victims of their own emotional inadequacies who live outside the code of the gentleman.

By the time of his death, Merriman had begun, as Oliver Edwards says,[83] "to develop certain faults" of style. Included among these are an occasional effect of staginess produced by a tendency to tell his story in short scenes, each of which ends in a minor climax, and a frequent melodramatic reliance on fate to bring these climaxes about. This technique may have resulted in Merriman's work, as it did in that of Dickens, from the fact that many of his stories were serialized prior to book publication. Many of the characters in the novels could be categorized as types, such as the man of action rather than words, the omniscient intriguer, the loyal servant, the sweet young heroine, and the man of the world. While the author's language is generally direct and simple, it is sometimes too liberally interspersed with sententious asides, a too-easy cynicism, and a fondness for archaic expressions and French speech tags. These faults were probably the unfortunate result of Merriman's desire to imitate his contemporaries by phrasing his story in the popular style.

CHAPTER 4

Miscellaneous Writings

IN addition to writing eighteen full-length novels in fifteen
years, Merriman published a number of short stories and two
books written jointly with his sister-in-law, Evelyn Beatrice Hall,
who wrote under the pseudonym Stephen G. Tallentyre. The
short stories were reissued after Merriman's death in a single volume called *Tomaso's Fortune and Other Stories.*

A catalogue issued by Maggs Brothers, the London booksellers,
lists for sale a few manuscript pages of what they refer to as the
conclusion of a novel, *The Great Game,* on which Merriman was
purported to have been working at the time he died.[1] There is
also a long short story, referred to in some of the author's correspondence[2] as "In Birling Deep." These additional items, in the
absence of evidence to the contrary, complete the corpus of Merriman's literary production.

I   *Essays*

From Wisdom Court, by Merriman and Stephen G. Tallentyre,
appeared in 1893, well before its author had published the books
which were to gain him his greatest popularity. He had already,
however, enjoyed enough success to cause him to give up business
permanently a year earlier in favor of literature; and this book
was, in a way, a mark of that success, for it was not in his customary vein of romantic adventure.

In this first collaborative effort, Merriman and Miss Hall offered
their readers a series of informal essays loosely tied together by
the imaginary convention which presented the authors as two de-
tached and contemplative observers of life offering their comments on the passing scene. The result is a collection of remarks
on a wide variety of subjects. These philosophical fragments are

expressed gracefully and unpretentiously, conveying to the reader the impression that he is listening to a cultivated and witty conversationalist.

Since these pieces were probably intended for publication in various periodical sources before being issued as a book, there is little internal unity except that provided by the conventional framework of the dispassionate observer of life. If the collection is read in conjunction with Merriman's novels, however, there is considerable unity—and consistency—between the viewpoints to be found in this volume and those in his other work. Here, as in the novels, are to be found the author's eulogies of individualism, honor, and self-reliance; his faith in the sense of duty; his satirical view of Darwinism; his distrust of schemes for social reform; his ridicule of the bluestocking; his conviction of the evanescence of romantic love; and the half-ironical dismay with which he contemplates the rapidly rising middle class.

In the paper entitled "On Courage," Merriman develops the theme that the degree of courage with which a person faces a given situation is directly proportional to the extent to which that person is dependent upon his own resources: "But best of all is the 'one man' courage—the single-handed, the self-reliant. This is the species most frequently met in the civilized world . . . In a higher grade of life this courage produces explorers, mountaineers, big game hunters and soldiers of fortune" (194–95).[3]

As a guide for the proper channeling of this sort of individual fearlessness, a man must adopt a purpose in life. This is the message of the essay "On Purpose." The purpose here spoken of is the sense of duty that motivated Merriman's most admirable character creations. Theodore Trist, Jack Meredith, Karl Steinmetz, Prince Paul Alexis, Reginald Cartoner, Wanda Bukaty, Sergeant Barlasch, Frederick Conyngham, Tony Cornish—all of these accomplished their objectives because of their dedication to duty and because they had the courage to persevere in the performance of that duty. Their opponents fail, almost invariably, because they are deficient in this sense of duty or because they allowed other considerations to divert them from duty. Purpose leads to success only if it is followed undeviatingly, but "If a man have purpose in life—a real strong purpose which never leaves him night or day, in joy or sorrow, in work or play—that man will, in all probability (say ten chances to one), attain his purpose before laying the things of this world aside." [4]

Merriman feared the rapid and unsettling expansion of scientific interest in the latter half of the nineteenth century. His attitude was apparently rooted in the belief that science was challenging the older and, to him, happier way of doing things. But more than this, he feared its leveling effect which would, he felt, destroy individualism. This attitude is discernible in the essay "On Honour and Glory."

For much the same reasons that he feared the inroads of science, Merriman distrusted schemes for social reforms. On the evidence of the novels, he felt that most such schemes were concocted by those who were primarily concerned with lining their own pockets. Beyond this, there was the implication that, even with the best motives, these plans tended to regiment people and to destroy the individual's self-reliance. He respected those who accomplished self-improvement, but refused to countenance the ideas of those who sought to spoon-feed people *en masse.*

The essay "On Girl" [5] praises the simple, uncomplicated, and completely feminine woman. Nothing but scorn is expressed for girls who make a fetish of learning or who affect intellectualism. Those who go in heavily for sports, who have a "mission," or who "suffer from inanity" are found equally objectionable. The redoubtable Julia Mangles in *The Vultures* is the author's most successful portrait of the woman with a mission, while Señora Barenna of *In Kedar's Tents* and the Countess Lanovitch in *The Sowers* characterize social inanity.

Although Merriman tended to idealize women, especially in depicting the heroines of his novels, he consistently avoids the portrayal of romantic love. There are no idyllic raptures in his novels; his heroes and heroines must be content to express their quiet affections in meaningful glances. In many of his works he hints at his belief that romantic love—love that does not face up to realities and responsibilities—is more apt to result in misery than in happiness. In "On Love" this hint becomes assertion, and full recognition is given to the compromise that is an inevitable part of living and loving.

In other essays in this volume Merriman reveals himself as one who is fully aware of the foibles and fancies of the English gentry. His attitude toward the upper middle-class society is generally somewhat akin to that of the adolescent who is both proud and ashamed of his parents. The essay "On Our Birthplace" expresses with gentle irony the growing concern over the changing nature of that society.[6]

The ideas selected from this relatively early book of essays are those which are voiced most often, in considerably amplified form, in the later novels. In fact, it may very possibly be that many of these slight but pleasant essays contained the first tentative statements of some of his major themes. Although the philosophy in these pieces is not profound, it is sound; and the expression of it is generally entertaining in spite of an occasional archness.

II *Character Sketches*

The Money Spinner and Other Character Notes, again by Merriman and Tallentyre, appeared in 1896 and is described as being composed of notes reprinted from the *Cornhill* magazine of the years 1893, 1894, and 1895. Although the book was originally intended to consist of the collaborative efforts of Merriman and Miss Hall, only a few are actually from the pen of Merriman.[7] The book contains twenty-three character sketches of such types as The Money Spinner or financier, The Nurse, The Scholar, The Mother, My Lord, The Laborer, The Squire, The Beauty, The Child, The Spinster, The New Woman, and The Farmer. Obviously, the authors must have intended to encompass all levels and conditions of men—to examine representatives from all the social strata.

Since these sketches are specifically called "character notes," their undeveloped and fragmentary nature is scarcely surprising, but they are dramatically convincing. Looked at as notes for future expansion, these pieces are interesting because many of them contain the germinal idea for some of Merriman's more successful characters. They are equally interesting as examples of the "characters" in the genre of character writing which was especially popular in the seventeenth century. Although these notes are only the raw material of fiction, certain of them have an extensive internal narrative pattern; but there is no attempt at any narrative thread to link the sketches with each other. The sketches are written so as to emphasize the most salient feature of the individual character being described. While many of the figures are thus only roughed in, others, by virtue of their reaction to the narrative situation in which they are placed, become well enough developed to engage the reader's sympathies.

Typical of this group is the financier in the title piece of the book, "The Money Spinner." Presented as an example of the type of entrepreneur who can make money but cannot enjoy the things it provides, he is contrasted against his children who are oriented toward enjoyment of money but cannot make it. The children are rather ashamed of their father and his common origins in Clapham. They fill the house with their fashionable friends and neglect the old man who understands neither them nor their friends. Even the wife, who married him for his money, has long since achieved her objective and deserted him. The Money Spinner's senile bids for attention are coldly rejected by the children because they feel that sentimentality betrays their bourgeois background.

The old man falls ill, much to the annoyance of his daughter, who feels that this illness may interrupt her plans for a party. She goes shopping, promising to bring a doctor back with her; but her father dies long before the doctor appears. The Money Spinner dies as desolately as he has lived, for only his butler, who is paid to be there, is present at his deathbed. After indulging in a stylish period of mourning, the children resume their normally vacuous and purposeless lives.

"The Nurse" is a study of a fanatically devoted child's nurse who stays with her young charge through a severe illness, even though she learns that the brother, whose expenses at Oxford she pays with great personal sacrifice, is expected to die. Her devotion to duty is rewarded, for both her patient and her brother recover.

In "The Labourer," an old working man, simple and faithful in his humble duties, dates all his reminiscences by incidents that occurred during his and his dead wife's married life. He dies as quietly and unassumingly as he has lived, comforted with a vision of his wife's presence.

"The Peasant" recounts how an old country woman zealously devotes herself to her slightly demented daughter. Eventually, the girl marries, but her husband deserts her. The old woman never deviates from her parental duty, but spends the rest of her life in protecting the girl, in expiation of the fancied crime of bringing a daft child into the world.

In addition to a group of such sketches as the foregoing, which are designed to underscore the importance of a dedication to duty, the book contains a number of pieces that point out the damage to human personality when the individual, lacking this sense of responsibility, is completely self-centered. Among these is "The Beauty," a worldly woman of thirty-seven, beautiful and heartless, who looks upon her husband as a fool and considers him beneath her. It pleases her vanity to act the part of nurse during his final illness; but, after his death, she begins to lose her beauty and seeks desperately but unavailingly for medical aid to preserve it. Finally, she comes to the bitter realization that this final prop to her vanity is irretrievably gone.

In the same category is "The Bad Penny," a young man who fails at Cambridge and throws himself upon the indulgence of his parents, knowing that they will accept his specious self-justifications. He decides to farm in Canada, but soon returns home, a failure for the second time. When he is eventually discharged from a position of trust for forgery, the boy's parents are forced to accept the realization of both their son's guilt and their own failure in fulfilling their parental duty.

A third group of these sketches is devoted mainly to satire, not of individuals but of ideas. In this respect, the sketches are more in the nature of essays than of character portrayals. Many of these satirical barbs were aimed at the inroads of feminism, a word that was, so far as Merriman was concerned, an unpleasant antonym for feminine, and hence inimical to romantic love. "Intellecta" concerns the "new" intellectual woman, who loves knowledge for its own sake, but does nothing with it. In "The Practical Woman," a woman becomes so enamored of practicality that she destroys the romance in her married life. Undaunted by this, she raises her infant son by a system so rigorously practical that the child dies. "The New Woman" is a critique of the new "mannish" woman who seeks to usurp man's place. Her efforts, like those of Julia Mangles in *The Vultures*, are no less ridiculous than her appearance; and, in the author's opinion, she fails utterly in trying to prove woman's mission is something higher than bearing and rearing children.

Most of the remaining sketches in the book are variations on the themes developed in one or the other of the three categories outlined above. Like *From Wisdom Court, The Money Spinner* is a sort of source book for many of the novelist's ideas and characters. It is obvious, for instance, how Julia Mangles might have developed out of "Intellecta" and "The New Woman"; and the ideas concerning devotion to duty or the lack of it could very well have inspired the creation of many more of Merriman's most memorable characters. Whatever deficiencies *The Money Spinner* may have in originality, or style, it still serves a very useful purpose as a guide to its author's attitudes and philosophy.

Since *The Money Spinner* appeared at the height of Merriman's success, it received some critical attention, although generally the book was noted only among the lists of new publications. The *Academy,*[8] which reviewed it in the same way that it reviewed any of the author's publications, said that the book was reminiscent of the volumes of "Characters" that are a feature of seventeenth-century literature, a "form that is now obsolete." These notes are called "the raw material of fiction, crude abstractions." Considered as notes for future elaboration, "they have merit"; thrown thus together, they are not good. Some are brightly written; others are "marred by cheap wit and pathos." The reviewer singles out the portraits of the Money Spinner and the Nurse as being among the best.

III *Short Stories*

The nineteen stories included in the volume called *Tomaso's Fortune and Other Stories* were collected after Merriman's death and published in 1904. All of them had probably appeared previously in one or the other of the magazines which were ready to buy anything he wrote, long or short. Two of the stories, "A Parish" and "The Prodigal's Return," appeared in the *Cornhill*[9] in 1896. These two tales were reprinted from the *Cornhill* in *Littell's Living Age*[10] in the same year. A short story called "Of This Generation," which does not appear in *Tomaso's Fortune,* was also published in 1896 in another American magazine, *McClure's.*[11]

These latter two periodicals are among the sources in addition to those mentioned by Merriman himself in his earlier letter to his mother.

"Of This Generation" was probably mistakenly excluded from *Tomaso's Fortune*. In respect to style and finish, it is superior to many of the stories in this volume; and it has many of the typical Merriman touches. There are the superior English hero whose deceptive air of the dandy conceals great determination and ability, and the demure and beautiful, but intelligent heroine who is able to maintain her composure in the face of a crisis, emotional or otherwise. There is also the colorful foreign setting—this time in Munich. Finally, there are the author's ironical observations and commentaries. Lord Burdon's effectiveness as an ambassador is ascribed to the fact that "he knows so much to the discredit of his neighbor—the surest means to success." [12] An unidentified member of the English peerage is described as "being well known for the length of his descent and the shortness of his comprehension." [13]

Merriman's success with the periodicals did not come without a struggle. A series of letters which he wrote over the years 1890 to 1892 to the publishers of *Blackwood's Magazine*[14] is chiefly concerned with his efforts to place with them another long short story which also does not appear in the *Tomaso* collection. In the correspondence, Merriman refers to this story as a one-volume novel, under the title "In Birling Deep." Although the tale was not accepted by *Blackwood's*, it is reported to have been published anonymously in 1896 by Richard Bentley and Sons in *Temple Bar*.[15]

Merriman's letters to *Blackwood's* refer to the fact that the magazine rejected two other stories of his, "Judged" and "Haunted Hand," but it did eventually publish "Sister" in 1892, probably one of the most successful of the stories included in *Tomaso's Fortune*. Neither "Judged" nor "Haunted Hand" appears in this collection. Although it was not published as a book until 1896, *Roden's Corner* must have been ready in manuscript as early as 1892, for, again according to these letters, it was refused for serialization in *Blackwood's* in that year.

Many of the stories in *Tomaso's Fortune* are quite similar in structure to the character sketches that appeared in *The Money Spinner*. Others have plots that are too complicated for entirely successful handling within the limits of the short story. Those which show the best balance in these respects are perhaps "Tomaso's Fortune," "Sister," "The Tale of a Scorpion," "The Mule," "At the Front," "In the Track of the Wandering Jew," and "Through the Gate of Tears."

Because certain of these stories are concerned with the experiences of various individuals engaged in the British Colonial Service, they are somewhat reminiscent of similar tales by Kipling. Others, which deal with adventures at sea, contain hints of Conrad. The Kipling influence seems particularly apparent in such tales of the British soldier in India as "In the Track of the Wandering Jew" and "Sister," while there are strong elements of Conrad in "Stranded," which relates the experiences of a man broken by the sea and by his own inordinate pride. At least one of the stories, "In a Caravan," with its account of a trip in a gypsy wagon, has the appeal of a chapter from George Borrow.

Merriman frequently employs the surprise ending, and he is fond of displaying the violence of human nature against the authentically detailed and somnolent background of the sea and the countries in the area of the Mediterranean. He also sometimes demonstrates a surgical skill in cutting with a few swift strokes to the heart of the drama he wishes to present. Although this method is incisive and objective, it does tend to restrict the leisurely and natural development of character and incident to the extent that the story seems to be told in a series of arbitrarily selected, but highly dramatic, scenes. Such occasional abrupt transitions contribute to the feeling that fate plays a disproportionate role in motivating action. However, such figures as Tomaso, Juan Quereno in "The Mule," and Captain Dixon in "Stranded" are brought to disaster or near it by some innate natural trait. Tomaso's shyness causes him to lose a fortune and almost to lose his sweetheart as well; Quereno is a sacrifice to duty and loyalty; and Dixon is destroyed by his own selfish pride.

Aside from their technique, these stories are particularly interesting because they often contain the somewhat tentative outlines of certain characters who were developed more fully in the novels. Carl von Mendebach, the fiercely proud but open-hearted German student in "Golossa-a-l," suggests the origin of that citizen of the world, Karl Steinmetz, who is presented so effectively in *The Sowers.* The British secret agent, Reginald Cartoner, appears in "For Juanita's Sake," as intrepidly efficient and as self-contained as he is in *The Vultures,* but not nearly so convincing as a human being as he is in that work. The physician who acts as narrator of many of these stories has points in common with the popular conception of the Byronic hero. Sometimes he is a member of an Indian regiment on the outposts of empire; sometimes he is the ship's doctor and medico turned novelist, Mark Ruthine; but always there is the feeling that this aloof and analytical observer is an idealized projection of the author as a man who is apart from society because of a mystery or sorrow associated with his past. Dr. Ruthine is also used to good advantage in *From One Generation to Another.*

"In the Track of the Wandering Jew" is a story of British soldiers in India that compares favorably with many similar tales by Kipling. This is an account of the tragedy that comes to General Thurkow, the commander of an Indian outpost, because he allows a natural, paternal love to sway him from the path of his military duty. With a similar background, "Sister" is another in Merriman's series of accounts of military personnel on the Indian frontier. The "Sister" in the story is a field-hospital nurse who allows herself to be mistaken by a dying and delirious British soldier for the girl he has left behind so that his last moments may be happy.

At least two of the characters in "Stranded" could have originated in Conrad's fertile imagination. One of these is Captain Dixon, a merchant-marine officer; the other is Stoke, his first mate. Captain Dixon has never made a mistake in seamanship until one night his ship runs aground in a fog bank with great loss of life including, presumably, that of the captain. Stoke takes charge of the rescue and salvage operations, and it is he who must take the news of her loss to the captain's beautiful and gentle widow. It soon becomes apparent that there is an unacknowledged attachment between Stoke and Mrs. Dixon. Eventually Stoke learns that there is another survivor of the wreck living in a little coastal village. When it is learned that this is Captain Dixon, whose nerve and mind have been broken by the accident, his wife joins him and they subsequently change their name and move to a new locality.

Told from the viewpoint of the ship's doctor, Mark Ruthine,

who has many points of resemblance to Conrad's Marlowe, "Through the Gate of Tears" concerns the experience of a poor parson's daughter, Norah Hood, who is traveling to one of the British colonies as the promised wife of a planter whom she has never seen. Aboard ship, she and a soldier, Mark Fenn, fall deeply in love. Realizing she can neither break the social and moral code nor disappoint the family depending on her in England, Norah commits suicide by drinking a drug taken from the doctor's cabinet. This situation, which could easily be oversentimentalized, is handled by Merriman with great restraint and objectivity.

Completely unencumbered by plot, "In a Caravan" is a simple narrative account of a trip through the English countryside in a gypsy wagon. More akin to the familiar essay than to the short story, it is written with great charm and quiet humor. The format also gives the author ample opportunity to exercise his descriptive powers, as in this passage on the joys of gypsying:

And the joy of the caravaneer was ours. This joy is not like the joy of other men. For the high-road, the hedgerows, the birds, the changing sky, the ever-varying landscape, belong to the caravaneer. He sits in his moving home and is saturated with the freedom of the gipsy without the haunting memory of the police, which sits like Care on the roof of the gipsy van. Book on lap, he luxuriates on the forecastle when the sun shines and the breeze blows soft noting idly the passing beauty of the scene, returning peaceably to the printed page. When rain comes, as it sometimes does in an English summer, he goes inside and gives a deeper attention to the book, while Parker drives and gets wet. Getting wet is one of Parker's duties. And through rain and sunshine he moves on ever, through the peaceful and never dull—the incomparable beauty of an English pastoral land. The journey is accomplished without fatigue, without anxiety; for the end of it can only be the quiet corner of a moor, or some sleepy meadow. Speed is of no account—distance immaterial. The caravaneer looks down with indifference upon the dense curiosity of the smaller towns; the larger cities he wisely avoids.[16]

Since the book appeared a few months after Merriman's death, reviews of *Tomaso's Fortune* paid passing tribute to this fact, as well as to the author's reputation with the reading public. The *Academy*[17] added that "most of these stories are really mere suggestions or rough sketches." The author, however, was complimented for his light touch and his ability to handle such slight incidents. These "small slices of life," concluded the reviewer, are "not exciting" but they "give pleasure."

The *Athenaeum*[18] allots some space to balancing Merriman's faults against his virtues as a writer, but it finds that the short-story form does not suit the author. He "needed time to develop plot, incident to show character, and room for local color." Some of the stories are called slight, others are said to "go too fast for the author's style." The critical conclusion is that the stories are "interesting because they are Merriman's," but they "will not add to his reputation."

CHAPTER 5

Evaluation and Summary—
Merriman's Stature

WHEN Merriman finished his final novel, *The Last Hope*, in
1903, he was probably looking forward to another twenty
or thirty years as a productive writer. For the preceding fifteen
years, since the publication of *Young Mistley*, there had been no
diminution in his literary output. He had been represented in the
publishers' lists by one or more books for each of those years. But
for the unfortunate result of his appendectomy, there is no reason
to assume that his inventiveness and his facility at telling a tale
would have failed him for many years to come. His reputation
with the reading public was firmly established, a fact attested by
the volume of his sales. A comparison of his later with his earlier
novels demonstrates that he was steadily growing and developing
in his handling of themes and techniques.

Since Merriman always rigorously eschewed the role of the literary lion, he was perhaps not unduly affected by the fact that the
critics of his own time were scarcely ever more than lukewarm
toward him. While they recognized the author's appeal and technical skill, they were disinclined to probe beneath the romantic or
conventional exterior of the novels. On the few occasions when
such sub-surface inspection did occur, the critic, as in the case of
Roden's Corner, was apt to point out the unsuitability of Merriman's tendency to mingle realistic and romantic themes. Even the
few later writers who discuss Merriman's work tend to be satisfied
with the mere application of the technical yardstick. Writing in
1957, Oliver Edwards says, *à propos* of the author's early death,

We can regret it for the man. We can doubt whether a more normal
span of activity would have added much to his fame. He matured
quickly; he even began to develop certain faults. His search for variety
of setting and subjects would inevitably have tended to peter out. He

was not likely to have bettered *In Kedar's Tents, The Velvet Glove, Flotsam,* and *The Sowers.* As it is, the fourteen volumes he chose to survive are an adequate, comprehensive, and durable memorial.[1]

On the other hand, Mr. Edwards does call attention to the Aristotelian concept of the character of Harry Wylam in *Flotsam.* Wylam's "tragedy was born with him; it was in his character." The book closes unhappily for Harry and Miriam, but there is, as Mr. Edwards says, "a certain sense of fulfillment."

Frank Swinnerton is an enthusiastic and articulate champion of Merriman's work. The very title of Swinnerton's often cited article in *John O'London's Weekly* calls Merriman the "Master of Romance." This title is in itself high praise, but it implies its own limitations so far as the subject is concerned. Appreciative as Mr. Swinnerton is of Merriman's abilities to depict courage, to weave an engrossing plot, to celebrate the simple virtues, to dramatize a situation, and to recreate a foreign scene, there is the inevitable feeling that, with all these excellences, he is not to be regarded as a "serious" novelist, within the generally understood meaning of that term. In short, Merriman is an expert craftsman, writing entertainingly and appealingly of "an earlier generation, before smartness had become the vogue," whose books "will continue to be read, re-read, and preserved for their peculiar qualities for several decades." [2] No deeper significance is accorded to him.

Malcolm Elwin saw influences of French Naturalism in Merriman's work. He also noted the author's conscious effort to excise from his books any material that might be deemed superfluous to the plot. It was Elwin too who remarked upon the author's application of psychology to romance, especially as this is evidenced in *Flotsam.* Both Elwin and Edwards, however, seem to have missed the many other examples of psychological character studies to be found in Merriman's novels. Like many of the critics of Merriman's own time, Elwin mentions the sharp delineation of characters and strong plots exhibited by the novels, although he feels that many of the principal characters lacked originality. In spite of this defect, writes Elwin, "Merriman achieved his effects by the skillful play of character upon character; the incidents of his narratives were the inevitable results of the coming into contact and conflicting interests of individuals." [3] The books are commended for their "genuine local color and atmosphere," and the author's language is called "direct and simple, continental in tone, but undistinguished." Elwin attributes Merriman's facility as a writer to the fact that "He followed Trollope's practice of planning his novels, with a synopsis of every chapter, before starting to write, and his manuscripts are said to contain few alterations or erasures." [4]

As has been pointed out, the critics who were contemporary with Merriman were perhaps less generous with their praise than the more recent ones. Just after Merriman's death, the *Outlook* [5] printed an obituary note of appreciation which was rather typical of such notices at that time. The reviewer comments on the fact that Scott was always governed by "a spirit of personal reserve and modesty." He is labeled a "born story-teller" with an unusual ability to construct plausible plots. While his character creations had life and movement, Scott "never went very deeply below the surface" in presenting these figures. His most significant contribution, in the *Outlook's* opinion, was his marked success in discovering "new ideas for use in fiction," as evidenced particularly in *The Sowers, Roden's Corner, The Vultures,* and *With Edged Tools.* Despite a certain unevenness "in quality," the "average of interest" in his stories "was decidedly large." Obituaries in the *Academy* [6] and the *Times* [7] spent much less time in analysis. The former publication did little more than contrast Scott's retiring nature with his popularity with the reading public; the latter emphasized primarily the social significance of the author's life and death.

In 1897, when Scott's career as a writer was already more than half over, the *Academy* [8] printed "Some Younger Reputations," which included an appraisal of "Mr. Henry 'Seton Merriman.' " This is probably the most extensive and most serious consideration of Scott as an artist to appear during his lifetime. The reviewer opens his discussion by posing this question: "Is Merriman one of the great, or only one of the second rate?" His conclusion is that it is still too early for a definite answer, but the fact that the question could be asked at all is an indication of the noteworthy present and possible future progress of the author. "The author," continues the reviewer, "writes so well one is disappointed that he does not write better." The male characters "are real flesh and blood creations." The scenery is described as vivid, the dialogue is called "concise and witty," and the plots are "well constructed." While the author is characterized as "intensely patriotic," he is judged to be not so "patent" in this respect as Kipling. Merriman's heroes "can go anywhere, do anything," and their creator "writes as an English gentleman should talk in mixed company. Yet," the article continues, "a novelist may have all these qualities and remain second rate." Merriman is further described as being "too fond of taking the reader aside, like Thackeray, for a cynical or trite comment on the story situation." The most serious accusation made against him is that he "shows no deep thought on great problems of existence." Publishers and editors are cautioned by the reviewer not to hurry Merriman, but to give him time "to write and edit his stories severely," for he may thus "justify his promise and achieve true literary work." The alternative with which the estimate concludes is that "Otherwise, he [Merriman] will remain one of the most agreeable of ephemeral romancers."

This analysis of Merriman's work presents a more objective assessment of his artistic contribution than most of his notices; but, like that of the others, the *Academy* reviewer's appreciation did not go much deeper than Merriman's surface pyrotechnics as evidenced by his skill in plotting, description, and character creation. The truth is that Merriman's technical facility probably made the whole business of tale telling look deceptively easy. As Elwin reminds us too, "The new generation—Wells, Bennett, and Galsworthy—would not concede that art could achieve wide popularity in the nineties, hence Merriman's artistic reputation suffered." [9] Merriman's avoidance of the light of publicity also made him virtually a figure of anonymity with the reviewers. Since he never made the slightest gesture to interpret his own work, it is not surprising that the critics on the periodicals, always pressed for time to keep up with the current crop of novels, might miss the theses underlying the surface brilliance of the style.

I *Merriman's Themes*

As in the case of many of those whose fictional product is highly entertaining, Merriman's ideas are difficult to come by. His frequent use of irony, moreover, might cause the hasty reader to conclude that such a writer could move no more serious purpose than to beguile his readers. While it is thus understandable that a reviewer might be misled into stating that an author "shows no deep thought on great problems of existence," the statement is pretty wide of the mark so far as Merriman is concerned.

Merriman did, in fact, express a great deal of thought on many aspects of the problems of existence. Some of these thoughts are stated directly in interpolated passages or in asides to the reader; many of them are also conveyed indirectly by the manner in which a character responds to a situation. While it could not be claimed, perhaps, that he either developed or intended to develop a philosophical system, much of what he has to say about life and living is as applicable to our own time as it was to his.

The major themes employed by Merriman to express his philosophy can be roughly categorized as national, international, social, or psychological in nature. Although these have been examined in detail in connection with the discussion of the novels, it might be well to recapitulate in order to establish a pattern for the author's thought. Since ideas that are national in scope inevitably affect one's international views, there cannot be a sharply defined division between these areas in Merriman's case. Similarly, the individual mind is a part of the mass mind; hence, the boundaries of Merriman's psychology are often inextricably fused with those of his sociology. Viewed through the perspective of his fictional themes, moreover, the author's opinions reflect the attitudes of his contemporaries.

In respect to the national-international category, Merriman was a firm adherent of the Empire. This is apparent in almost all of his books, but it is particularly emphasized in those novels whose settings are in India at or near the time of the Mutiny. Both *From One Generation to Another* and *Flotsam* express approval of British policy in India. This satisfaction with the monarchy and the Empire is further emphasized in *The Vultures*, which contrasts the evils that arise under tyranny with the advantages pertaining to a benevolent monarchy. *With Edged Tools* is a sort of tribute to the men who extended the boundaries of the British Empire even as Meredith and Oscard established their own Simiacine empire in the hostile African jungles. *With Edged Tools*, like the books dealing with India, also recognized the Briton's willingness to "bear the white man's burden" in unenlightened areas, whatever the cost may be. *Prisoners and Captives* and *In Kedar's Tents* exhibit the Englishman operating in a similar capacity in Russia and Spain, respectively. These last two books, together with *The Sowers* and *The Vultures,* are the works in which the author states most forcefully his opposition to tyranny and reveals his compassion for the less fortunate peoples of the world. *Roden's Corner* shows the same compassion for the lower classes at the mercy of the upper classes.

Many of Merriman's books portray the evils engendered by hatred and warfare. *The Grey Lady* explores the corrosion of human character under the influence of long-standing hatred, and *The Isle of Unrest* shows the far-reaching tragedy and unhappiness brought about by a feud. *From One Generation to Another* is a sort of object lesson in the destructive effects of vengeance. *Young Mistley, Suspense, Prisoners and Captives, The Slave of the Lamp, In Kedar's Tents, The Velvet Glove, The Vultures,* and *Barlasch of the Guard* underscore the futility and waste of warfare as a means of settling international disputes.

The author's conviction that the British gentleman is a superior human being emerges unmistakably from these books. Winyard Mistley, Theodore Trist, Christian Vellacott, Jack Meridith, James Agar, Prince Paul Alexis (who is half British), Frederick Conyngham, Anthony Cornish, and Reginald Cartoner are Merriman's ideal heroes; and each one, irrespective of his station in life, represents the essential qualities of gentlemanliness. They are patriotic and dedicated individuals; they persevere to the point of stoicism, are completely unselfish, and are possessed of great charm, kindliness, and human sympathy. They are fascinated by the lure of adventure in strange places, and, in order that their pursuit of adventure may appear more natural, several of them are presented as secret agents, soldiers, or foreign correspondents. If available biographical evidence may be accepted as a criterion, all of them are projections of their creator, with his characteristic likes and dislikes. Thus Merriman is able to infuse his fictional creations with his own enthusiasm for travel and high adventure.

Psychologically and sociologically, Merriman's attitudes were conditioned by the fact that the materialism of his own world constantly jarred against his idealized conception of the past. He would probably have preferred the era of knight errantry when the strong and forceful but compassionate individual could set things right without regard for class or caste, for special interest group or organization. His Humanism was strictly personal, regulated only by a strong sense of duty and a stoical willingness to accept whatever life had to offer. Because he believed that the age just prior to his own had offered more latitude to the individual, many of his novels were set in this period. His contempt for the thinkers and the esthetes and his respect for the men of action who do the world's work are particularly apparent in *The Phantom Future*, with its coterie of intellectuals, and in *Suspense*, which introduces the spineless esthete, William Hicks.

Merriman had great sympathy for the downtrodden, the unfortunate, and the exploited in the world; but he distrusted the various "schemes" and "plans" that were being advocated for their relief. His hatred of tyranny was balanced by a fear of revolution, as it is exemplified by the Nihilist groups in *Young Mistley* and in *The Sowers*, and by Kosmaroff in *The Vultures*. Such undisciplined groups, he felt, invariably fell, like the charity organizations, under the control of those who were motivated by opportunism and self-interest. Merriman's own prescription for the relief of the underprivileged was the natural process of evolution, aided by an entirely personal sort of charity administered unostentatiously in the Biblical sense. He felt too that education, not ladled out in indigestible doses to the masses, but properly apportioned to those who were ready to receive it, would help to alleviate life's inequities. The author's conception of true charity is represented by Prince Paul in *The Sowers*, who goes about incognito and provides his sick and starving peasants with medical attention and education while reproving them for their idleness. Sister Cecelia in *From One Generation to Another* and Von Holzen and Roden in *Roden's Corner*, on the other hand, illustrate the incalculable harm that may result when opportunism disguises itself as organized charity.

Merriman's orientation toward the concept of individualism and his attachment for the past probably contributed to his limited understanding of women. He respected women for their femininity and for their simple virtues of loyalty, honor, and dignity. Along with an earlier generation, he honored the ties of family and felt that woman's most important function in society was to serve as the focal point of the family unit. The heroines of his novels were, like the men whom they loved honorably and without affectation, dedicated to their duty and stoical in their acceptance of disappointment and tragedy. In fact, both men and women, antagonists as well as protagonists, have learned the very important lesson that living is a continual adjustment to change. The honorable characters accept all of life's compromises except those involving their principles; those less honorable, who compromise even with principle, accept the consequences without complaint. While Merriman's heroines are intelligent, they are never intellectual. The intellectual bluestocking was to him a curious anomaly who had no place in the world of his imagination, and he delighted in satirizing her through the media of a Julia Mangles in *The Vultures* or of an "Intellecta" in the story thus titled. But even worse than the militant feminist was the woman who used her femininity for strictly selfish purposes. The former were at worst nuisances; the latter were dangerous. Millicent Chyne in *With Edged Tools,* Mrs. Harrington and Agatha Ingham-Baker in *The Grey Lady,* and Etta Bamborough in *The Sowers* are properly punished for their greedy opportunism. Lena Wright in *Young Mistley,* Brenda Gilholme in *Suspense,* Dora Glynde in *From One Generation to Another,* Jocelyn Gordon in *With Edged Tools,* Dorothy Roden in *Roden's Corner,* Désirée Sebastian in *Barlasch of the Guard,* and Wanda Bukaty in *The Vultures* are, on the other hand, amply rewarded for their selfless and sincere devotion.

Since pressure groups of whatever origin threaten the sovereignty of the individual, Merriman naturally feared and distrusted them as potential disrupters of the status quo. For this reason, he took issue with the proponents of science and was occasionally scornful of Darwinism. A similar feeling in regard to militant racial and religious groups caused him to concentrate upon religion as a clue to character in both *The Velvet Glove* and *Slave of the Lamp,* which deal with the political machinations of the Jesuits. In *From One Generation to Another,* he concentrates upon race as a clue to character in depicting the Jewish archvillain, Seymour Michael.

Several commentators on Merriman's work have noticed, in *Flotsam,* and other books, his psychological interpretation of character. Harry Wylam is by no means the only one of Merriman's creations to be brought to disaster by a tragic fault in his psychic makeup. In *The Phantom Future,* Tom Valliant's premonitions about his health develop into an actual death wish which causes him to waste his talents and his life. Anna Agar's passion for vengeance in *From One Generation to Another* eventually destroys everything she values, and her communication of this passion to her son warps his life and indirectly brings about his death. Innate and overpowering greed ruins Victor Durnovo in *The Sowers,* Mrs. Harrington and the Ingham-Bakers in *The Grey Lady,* Etta Bamborough in *The Sowers,* Percy Roden and Otto Von Holzen in *Roden's Corner,* Seymour Michael in *From One Generation to Another,* the Vicomte De Clericy in *Dross,* and Colonel Gilbert in *The Isle of Unrest.* The lust for power ruins Claude de Chauxville in *The Sowers* and brings the Jesuits to grief in *The Slave of the Lamp* and *The Velvet Glove.* Luke Fitz Henry in *The Grey Lady* sacrifices his integrity to his consuming passion for Agatha.

II *Narrative Techniques*

A summary of Merriman's narrative techniques, as these have been examined in connection with the individual novels, might logically start with those qualities that impressed his contemporaries most forcibly. Among these, his methods of plot development are of great importance because he was widely acclaimed for his ability to tell an interesting story. In the majority of his books, the plots have some historical incident or series of incidents as a frame of reference. In *From One Generation to Another* and in *Flotsam* this incident is the Indian Mutiny. *Young Mistley, The Sowers, Prisoners and Captives,* and *The Vultures* get their impetus from the rise of the Nihilist movement and the agitations of various European peoples for relief from the oppression of the Russian czar. *In Kedar's Tents* and *The Velvet Glove* are built around the Spanish Carlist rebellions. The Franco-Prussian War furnishes the background for *The Isle of Unrest* and *Dross,* and Napoleon's invasion of Russia does a like service for *Barlasch of the Guard.* Some of the books—*The Phantom Future, Roden's Corner, With Edged Tools,* and *The Last Hope*—are not tied directly to any historical period.

Against this often historical and generally foreign background, groups of characters, some of them actual historical personages, are involved in a series of events that are complicated by intrigue and daring adventure. Woven into the plot fabric is at least one love story, the culmination of which coincides with the resolution of the main problem. Thus, the typical Merriman story is a combination of historical novel, adventure story, and romance.

The action of the author's stories is frequently begun in England, shifted to the foreign scene, and then transferred back and forth between the two locales. This necessitates constant change in point of view so that emphasis may be equalized between the characters on the home scene and those abroad. It also gives the author an opportunity to extend his own narrative and philosophical horizons by permitting him to interpret action and opinion from both the foreign and the domestic viewpoints. More importantly, such an arrangement contributes to the effectiveness of one of Merriman's most striking techniques—the dramatic arrangement of the scenes in his stories. The action is divided into a series of scenes much like those in a play, and they correspond roughly to the chapter divisions of the novel. Each of these chapter-scenes rises to a crescendo of interest that may be satisfied in the succeeding chapter; or, in order to heighten suspense, this satisfaction may be deferred for several chapters while other plot developments are brought up to date. All of these minor climaxes are directly involved with the ultimate denouement of the main plot of the story, except in some of the earlier novels where, in probable imitation of predecessors like Thackeray and Dickens, Merriman made rather wide use of subplots.

Merriman's success in adapting the techniques of the dramatist to the craft of the novel may have been the result of his previously mentioned interest and participation in amateur theatricals. This interest may also have been partially responsible for his skill in depicting characters and settings, for he saw both people and places with the dramatist's eye, picking out the most salient features of each unerringly. Merriman's habit of identifying characters in his novels by means of descriptive speech or action tags— Major White's "Thump 'em," Joseph Mangles' references to his sister "Joolie," John Turner's wry humor, or Cartoner's terseness— bespeak the dramatist. Playwright and poet are combined in his vivid and often lyrical descriptions of the settings of his books, settings that were the more authentic because they were places he had visited and known.

Merriman's facility at thus differentiating characters one from another was sometimes instrumental in producing stock figures, although his most heroic creations had their weaknesses and his blackest villains had not lost all contact with humanity. Prince Paul Alexis showed a lack of perception in respect to Etta Bamborough, and Claude de Chauxville demonstrated by his final act that his love for Etta was genuine. The author's slight tendency toward orotundity and formality of style in some of his early novels showed that he was, from the beginning, conscious of the sound, as well as the substance, of language.

Like many of his fellow novelists, Merriman was fond of speaking to his readers directly on occasion. The several examples of these asides already quoted illustrate how they provided him with a means, not only of sharing confidences about the story and the characters, but also of delivering philosophical opinions and satirical or ironic comments on the social structure and ideals of his time. His irony usually took the form of understatement, a device which he used exceptionally well. Time has validated the prophetic accuracy of many of his economic and political pronouncements, particularly those regarding Russia and certain Central European countries.

Merriman understood the importance of fate as an element in human decision and action, but the reader is generally prepared for the introduction of the unexpected by adequate foreshadowing. Thus the reader's credulity is not strained by such unusual events as the outcome of the charity swindle in *Roden's Corner*, the dramatic finale to the peasants' attack on the castle in *The Sowers*, or the success of Phillip Lamond's machinations in *Flotsam*. Merriman's descriptive powers seldom flagged in such scenes as the above. He seemed to have an uncanny faculty for choosing exactly the right details to yield the maximum authenticity and excitement; moreover, his customary device of beginning each chapter *in medias res* strengthened this effect. While these scenes of intense excitement are not too frequent in Merriman's work, they are masterfully handled when they do occur. Scenes of tragic violence, such as the theater fire and the fate of the Siberian refugees in *Prisoners and Captives*, General Vincente's last battle in *In Kedar's Tents,* the siege of Plevna in *Suspense,* and Napoleon's army at Borodino in *Barlasch of the Guard,* are detailed with realistic force and vigor.

III *Merriman and His Contemporaries*

Merriman wanted success as a writer. He was pleased to disclose to his mother and family the measure of his popularity with readers and the fact that editors were willing to publish almost anything he wrote. In view of his avoidance of all forms of personal publicity and the financial position of his family, it is unlikely that his desire for success stemmed from either a wish to be lionized or economic necessity. Perhaps his perseverance as a writer had its roots in a determination to prove that his father had been wrong in trying to force him to give up writing and go into business. It may have been that writing seemed to him the only feasible means by which he could indulge his own innate love of travel and adventure.

Whatever his reasons for adopting the profession, he approached writing seriously as one who, having something to say, deliberately chose the form that would assure a wide dissemination for his ideas. The serious purpose in even his earliest books has been pointed out. There is ample evidence too of his consciousness of technique. He demonstrated that he had definite artistic goals by applying the critical faculty to his own work and withdrawing certain of these early books from publication because he considered them "beneath his standard."

The romantic adventure story was one of the most popular literary forms of the day. A writer who desired popular success could hardly make a better choice than this medium. Merriman's idealistic vision of the past and his disgust with the materialism of his time probably gave him additional reasons for doing so. Among his contemporaries and rivals for popular favor, all of whom showed a similar fondness for the tale of romantic adventure, were his friend, Stanley J. Weyman; Rudyard Kipling; Sir Henry Rider Haggard; Sir Hall Caine; Anthony Hope; and Joseph Conrad. George Gissing, although primarily a Naturalist, also wrote a novel of international intrigue—*Veranilda.* Just as there are certain parallels between the work of Merriman and that of such predecessors as Thackeray and Dickens, there are similarities between Merriman's methods and those of his contemporaries.

Merriman shared with Hall Caine a taste for history and the dramatic incident. Both of them, too, were adept at conveying local color and at weaving a fascinating and exciting plot, but Caine departed much farther from the realm of actuality than Merriman did and his books, filled as they are with melodramatic horrors, are more akin to the Gothic Romances. They lack the realistic touches that link Merriman's stories to life.

Anthony Hope's best-known books, *The Prisoner of Zenda* and *Rupert of Hentzau,* are completely withdrawn from actual life because they deal with a completely imaginary country. Hence whatever social commentary they contain is solely applicable to conditions that exist only in his imagination. In some of his other books, however, he comes much closer to Merriman. The *Dolly Dialogues,* which records the conversations of a woman and the man she has jilted, illustrates that he had, like Merriman, extensive powers of observation concerning the fashions and foibles of society. An even more striking parallel between Hope and Merriman can be seen in Hope's *The God in the Car,* which, like *With Edged Tools,* deals with the adventures of company promotion in Africa.

Stanley Weyman's historical interests were more strictly confined than those of his traveling companion, Merriman. Weyman's most celebrated romances, *Under the Red Robe, Count Hannibal,* and *A Gentleman of France,* are all concerned with incidents in the history of France and with the adventures of certain imaginary soldiers of fortune associated with those incidents. *Under the Red Robe* deals with a projected uprising against Cardinal Richelieu and with the duelist, Gil de Berault, who is forced, despite his sympathies, to spy upon the opposition for the cardinal. The action of the other two books is involved with the struggles between the Huguenots and the Catholics in France. Like Merriman, Weyman is fascinated with the theme of espionage, but he makes spying a dirty business instead of emphasizing, as Merriman does, the skill and usefulness of the secret agent's profession. Weyman tells his story from multiple points of view, he gets to the heart of his story immediately, and he is able to sketch in a scene rapidly and convincingly. But, possibly because his stories are so far removed in time, his characters seldom seem to have any depth, and the locales prevent him from making any contributions as an interpreter of his time. Weyman does not share Merriman's reticence in dealing with a love scene. Merriman's lovers are content with a meaningful glance and a word or two; Weyman's suitors often grow extravagantly romantic in their declarations.

George Gissing's reputation rests on his realistic novels of the contemporary lower and middle classes, but in *Veranilda* he turned from this milieu to a romance of Rome under Justinian. The historical reconstruction of the sixth-century Roman Empire is meticulous in this book; but more interesting as a point of comparison with the work of Merriman is the fact that this story chronicles the activities of Marcian, a secret agent in the Greek service, who acts as a counter agent for the Goths because his sympathies lie in that direction. Marcian's divided allegiance is misunderstood by those who trusted him, and his life ends on a note of tragedy and disgrace. The beautiful Goth heroine, Veranilda, exhibits the qualities of womanly dignity, honor, and patience which Merriman's heroines represent.

At least one of Kipling's books demonstrates afresh that Merriman was fully aware of the literary tastes and trends of his time. *Kim* is a story filled with the panoply of Colonial India, encompassing every facet of its life, its customs, and its people. More significantly in respect to Merriman's work, it is the story of an English boy who, growing and developing against this background, accidentally becomes a spy for the British and is later educated for Her Majesty's Secret Service by the English in the Catholic college at Lucknow. Kipling's Indian canvas in *Kim* is much broader than Merriman's in *From One Generation to Another* or *Flotsam,* but the common interest in espionage methods is worth attention. In spite of their common fascination with the theme, Kipling, in contrast to Merriman, reveals in the last part of *Kim* his basic revulsion at his hero's vocation.

Kipling's journalistic style, though more abrupt than Merriman's, nevertheless reveals the same fascination with intrigue. Occasional references to the method by which intelligence information was collected illustrate Kipling's knowledge of the process, however much he disapproved of it. While Merriman's intelligence operatives take pride in the efficient execution of their tasks, Kim becomes more and more disillusioned and revolted at the underhanded work he must do. Under the influence of the example furnished by his gentle lama, he becomes so convinced of the evil nature of his activities that he is at length forced to cry out, "I am Kim. I am Kim; and what is Kim?" [10]

Rider Haggard's books range from documentary realism in *Cetywayo and His White Neighbours* to wildly imaginative tales of Gothic horror such as *Maiwa's Revenge* and *She*. Like Merriman, he was an inveterate traveler, and he used his knowledge of the world as a source for the scenes of his books. His most popular books were probably those set in Africa. His daughter Lilias records how necessary it was for Haggard to augment his income by his writing.[11] It may have been this need that caused him to abandon realism permanently in favor of the sensational romance. Merriman's quieter drama rarely ever approached the melodramatic horrors that were Haggard's stock in trade. Perhaps the nearest he ever came to rivaling this sort of thing was in his description of Durnovo's final appearance in *With Edged Tools*.

Haggard joined with Merriman in championing the British Empire and in recognizing the faults as well as the superiorities of his countrymen. He wrote on one occasion:

The rise of the British Empire in the teeth of the hamperings and opposition of British Statesmen and the elephantine obstinacy and stupidity of permanent Officials, is and always must remain one of the marvels of the world. Truly the Anglo-Saxon race is great. The folly and self-seeking of such creatures lost us America, but the genius of our blood, even when mixed, is going to bring it back into a closer and more enduring union.[12]

Haggard too, like Merriman, wrote with amazing facility. *King Solomon's Mines, Allan Quatermain, Jess,* and *She* were written in fourteen months,[13] but the nature of his plots and settings did not permit him to interpret the actual life of his time as Merriman did. Yet many of his characters, in spite of their highly imaginative adventures, were drawn from life,[14] as was true of Merriman's.

Joseph Conrad's novels feature many of the themes with which Merriman was most concerned—the psychological interpretation of character, adventure in strange lands, the lure of the sea, and even, in *The Secret Agent*, the interest in intelligence service. It has already been pointed out that one or more of these elements was present in almost everything that Merriman wrote, and the works of Conrad are too familiar to need cataloguing in this respect. Conrad's approach to adventure was realistic, but he could not prevent the atmosphere of Romance from coloring the whole. Consciously or not, Merriman's narrative method was the reverse of this process. His conception of adventure was romantic and idealistic, but his genuine interest in the inner forces that move people to action forced him to adopt, possibly against his will, many of the techniques of Realism. An interest and experience in many lands made both Conrad and Merriman adept at creating vivid and impressionistic settings for their books.

The comparisons with his fellow novelists have been made in an attempt to show that Merriman was completely aware of the literary trends of his time and that his peculiar combination of talents placed him often in the position of helping to formulate those trends. The accuracy of his social and political commentary, the soundness of his psychology in interpreting character, and his realistic creation of espionage and business environment place him very high in the group of contemporaries with whom he has been compared. Although his stature as an esthetic artist is not that of a Conrad, his stature as a creative novelist is, in the respects that have been mentioned, at least equal to that of many of his contemporaries, always excluding Conrad of course; and it has earned him an enduring place in the history of literature.

Merriman's own work offers sufficient evidence of his ability to use effectively the techniques and ideas that were shared by his contemporaries. In his particular application of the theme of espionage to the novel, he was a pioneer. Several of the writers who had preceded him, as well as many of his contemporaries, used elements of mystery and foreign intrigue in their work. The secret agent was no stranger to fiction. Earlier writers, however, were inclined to regard spying as a pretty dirty business, and they presented such protagonists either as victims of circumstance, or else exploited them as figures of sensationalism. Merriman's espionage agents were described realistically in terms of their intelligent contributions to interpretation of political behavior and its potentials. The intelligence operative became, under Merriman's skillful handling, a focal point of concentration for the author's probing of international tensions. Merriman has invested this figure, moreover, with such a wealth of detail as to personal habits and official activities that he emerges from the novels as a real human being. Just as Sherlock Holmes epitomizes all that is implicit in the term "private investigator," so might Reginald Cartoner be described as the literary prototype of the sympathetic, conscientious, and realistic secret agent as a literary hero.

Novelists who followed Merriman were quick to recognize the appeal of such a figure, especially because the uneasy international situation, which erupted eleven years after Merriman's death into World War I, added increasing importance and interest to the role of the secret agent. Thus Cartoner, by virtue of his creator's foresight, assumes his place as literary progenitor of John Buchan's Colonel Hannay and of Somerset Maugham's Ashenden.

Notes and References

Chapter One

1. Frank Swinnerton, "Master of Romance." Letters to Gog and Magog—*John O'London's Weekly*, LX (Dec. 14, 1951), 881.

2. Oliver Edwards, "A Sense of Duty." Talking of Books. London *Times* (Oct. 3, 1957).

3. London *Times* (Nov. 20, 1903).

4. Malcolm Elwin, *Old Gods Falling*. (New York, 1939), p. 275.

5. Copy of Certificate of Birth. General Register Office, Somerset House, London, July 3, 1957. *Dictionary of National Biography*. (London, 1912), Vol. III, p. 278.

6. From Ampney St. Peter, near Cirencester, Gloucestershire, Oct. 14, 1956.

7. Letter cited above.

8. Letter from Merriman to his mother, written from France, June 7, 1895. Contained in catalogue of Maggs Brothers, Booksellers, London.

9. Frederic Villiers, *Villiers, His Five Decades of Adventure*. (New York and London, 1920), Vol. II, pp. 193–94.

10. Letter from Frank Swinnerton, Old Tokefield, Cranleigh, Surrey, Aug. 28, 1956.

11. The Reverend G. Williams, "The Wisdom of Henry Seton Merriman." (Unpublished collection of memorabilia).

12. Letter from D. Greenall, Head of Information Department, Lloyd's, London, E.C. 1, Jan. 16, 1957.

13. *Dictionary of National Biography*, Vol. III, p. 278.

14. London *Times*, Nov. 29, 1903.

15. *Dictionary of National Biography*, Vol. III, p. 278.

16. In a letter from Mrs. Olive S. D'Arcy Hart, April 27, 1957.

17. The log was obtained through the kindness of Mrs. Denise Gibbs. © Mrs. Denise Gibbs.

18. Frederic Villiers, *op. cit.*, pp. 193–94.

19. Letter from Joseph Spurr, an associate of Scott's at Lloyd's, Dec. 11, 1956.

20. D. Greenall, letter cited.

21. By Mrs. Denise Gibbs. © Mrs. Denise Gibbs.

22. *Dictionary of National Biography*, Vol. III.

23. Letter from Miss Dorothy Rushton (Scott's cousin), Bickenhall Mansions, London, W. 1, Jan. 29, 1957.

24. Supplied by J. G. Hamilton Jackson (Scott's godson), Brigadoon, Buxted, Sussex.

25. *John O'London's Weekly* (Jan. 2, 1952).

26. J. G. Hamilton Jackson, letter cited.

27. *Dictionary of National Biography*, Vol. III.

28. *John O'London's Weekly* (Jan. 2, 1952).

29. London *Times*. Obituary (Nov. 20, 1903).

30. Letter from the National Central Library, London, W.C. 1, May 29, 1956.

31. J. G. Hamilton Jackson, letter cited.

32. Dorothy Rushton, letter cited.

33. *Ibid.*

34. Quoted by Malcolm Elwin, *op. cit.*, p. 278.

35. Malcolm Elwin, *op. cit.*, p. 278.

36. *Dictionary of National Biography*, Vol. III. Stanley J. Kunitz and Howard Haycraft. *British Authors of the Nineteenth Century* (New York, 1936), p. 543.

37. Quoted in a letter from Mrs. Olive S. D'Arcy Hart, London, W. 11, Oct. 14, 1957.

38. Frederic Villiers, *op. cit.*, p. 194.

39. Quoted by the Rev. G. Williams, *op. cit.*

40. Villiers, *op. cit.*, pp. 193–94.

41. Elwin, *op. cit.*, p. 275.

42. Kunitz and Haycraft, *op. cit.*, p. 543.

43. *Dictionary of National Biography*, Vol. III, pp. 278–79.

44. Dorothy Rushton, letter cited.

45. Letter from Mrs. Denise Gibbs. Ampney St. Peter, Gloucestershire. Oct. 14, 1956.

46. J. G. Hamilton Jackson, letter cited.

47. Joseph Spurr, letter cited.

48. Letter from Richard E. Webb, Reference and Library Division, British Information Services, Washington, D. C., May 1, 1957.

49. Letter to Mrs. Hart from T. Hinkler, Treasury Chambers, London, S.W. 1, Jan. 9, 1957.

50. Picture supplied by J. G. Hamilton Jackson.

51. Dorothy Rushton, letter cited. J. G. Hamilton Jackson, letter cited.

52. *Dictionary of National Biography*, Vol. III.

53. Oliver Edwards, *op. cit.*

54. Copy of Entry of Death, General Register Office, Somerset House, London.

55. *Dictionary of National Biography*, Vol. III.

56. Last Will and Testament, Oct. 14, 1896.

57. Quoted in a letter from Mrs. Hart, London W. 11, Oct. 14, 1957.

58. Mrs. Hart, letter cited.

59. From a clipping from Maggs Brothers' catalogue, forwarded by Mrs. Hart.

Chapter Two

1. He gave up business entirely in 1892.

2. Dorothy Rushton, letter cited.

3. See Malcolm Elwin, *op. cit.*, p. 274.

4. Malcolm Elwin, *op. cit.*, p. 275.

5. Edward Wagenknecht, *Cavalcade of the English Novel* (2nd ed. New York, 1954), p. 565.

6. Malcolm Elwin, *op. cit.*, p. 275.

7. *The Academy*, XXXIII (Feb. 4, 1888), 76.

8. Quoted by Frank Swinnerton, *op. cit.*

9. Henry Seton Merriman, *Young Mistley* (New York, 1899).

10. Henry Seton Merriman, *The Phantom Future* (New York, 1888).

11. Henry Seton Merriman, *Suspense* (New York, 1899).

12. Henry Seton Merriman, *Prisoners and Captives* (New York, 1899).

Chapter Three

1. Henry Seton Merriman, *The Slave of the Lamp* (New York, 1903).

2. *Athenaeum* (May 7, 1892), No. 3367, p. 599.

3. Henry Seton Merriman, *From One Generation to Another* (New York, 1892).

4. London *Bookman*, III (Oct., 1892–March, 1893), 130.

5. *Athenaeum* (March 25, 1893), No. 3413, p. 373.

6. *Ibid.*

7. Malcolm Elwin, *op. cit.*, p. 277.

8. *Loc. cit.*

9. Henry Seton Merriman, *With Edged Tools* (New York, 1894).

10. *Saturday Review*, LXXXII (Aug. 22, 1896), 191.

11. *Athenaeum* (May 12, 1894), No. 3472, p. 609.

12. *Academy*, LII (July–Dec., 1897), 490.

13. See volumes XVIII, XXI, XXII, and XXIV of the *Cornhill* for the years cited.

14. See letter cited in Chapter I.

15. Henry Seton Merriman, *The Grey Lady* (New York, 1895).

16. *Athenaeum* (Jan. 11, 1896), No. 3559, p. 50.

17. *Literary Weekly*, XXVII (Mar. 21, 1896), 92.

18. *Literary Weekly*, XXIX (June 11, 1898), 183.

19. *Ibid.*

20. Henry Seton Merriman, *The Sowers* (New York, 1899).

21. See *Athenaeum* (Oct. 1, 1898), No. 3701, p. 449.

22. Henry Seton Merriman, *The Sowers.*

23. *Saturday Review*, LXXXII (Aug. 22, 1896), 191.

24. See Dorothy Rushton, letter cited. Apparently Miss Rushton also believes that her cousin did not visit Russia.

25. *Athenaeum* (Mar. 14, 1896), No. 3568, p. 341.

26. *Bookman* [American], III (Feb., 1896), 56–57.

27. *Academy*, XLIX (Jan.–June, 1896), 302.

28. *Critic*, XXVIII (Feb. 8, 1896), 93.

29. Malcolm Elwin, *op. cit.*, p. 276.

30. *Loc. cit.*

31. Oliver Edwards, *op. cit.*

32. Henry Seton Merriman, *Flotsam* (New York, 1896).

33. *Academy*, L (July–Dec. 1896), 257–58.

34. *Athenaeum* (Aug. 15, 1896), No. 3590, p. 219.

35. *Saturday Review*, LXXXII (Aug. 22, 1896), 191.

36. Malcolm Elwin, *op. cit.*

37. Frank Swinnerton, *op. cit.*

38. Edward Wagenknecht, *Cavalcade of the English Novel* (New York, 1954), p. 565.

39. Oliver Edwards, *op. cit.*

40. Henry Seton Merriman, *In Kedar's Tents* (New York, 1903).

41. *Dial*, XXIII (Dec. 16, 1897), 391.

42. *Saturday Review*, LXXXIV (Oct. 30, 1897), 474.

43. *Ibid.*

44. *Dial, loc. cit.*

45. *Bookman* [American], VI (Sept. 1897–Feb. 1898), 351–52.

46. *Academy*, LII (July–Dec. 1897), 490.

47. *Athenaeum* (Nov. 6, 1897), No. 3654, p. 629.

48. Frank Swinnerton, *op. cit.*

49. *Bookman* [English], XV (Oct. 1898–Mar. 1899), 30–31.

50. Henry Seton Merriman, *Roden's Corner* (New York, 1898).

51. *Athenaeum* (Oct. 1, 1898), No. 3701, p. 449.

52. *Outlook*, LX (Nov. 12, 1898), 60.

53. *Dial,* XXV (Dec. 16, 1898), 457.
54. *Academy,* LIV–LV (Sept. 24, 1898), 296.
55. *Harper's,* XCVII (Supplement, October, 1898), 4.
56. Cornelius Weygandt, *A Century of the English Novel* (New York, 1925), p. 325.
57. *Dictionary of National Biography,* Vol. III (London, 1912), pp. 278–79.
58. Henry Seton Merriman, *Dross* (Chicago, 1899).
59. Malcolm Elwin, *op. cit.,* p. 277.
60. Henry Seton Merriman, *The Isle of Unrest* (New York, 1900).
61. *Bookman* [English], XIX (Oct. 1900–Mar. 1901), 61.
62. *Bookman* [American], XII (Sept. 1900–Feb. 1901), 584.
63. *Athenaeum* (Sept. 29, 1900), No. 3805, p. 408.
64. *Academy,* LIX (July–Dec. 1900), 242, 416.
65. See Oliver Edwards, *op. cit.,* and Malcolm Elwin, *op. cit.*
66. Henry Seton Merriman, *The Velvet Glove* (New York, 1901).
67. *Academy,* LXIII (Jan.–June 1902), 493.
68. *Athenaeum* (Jan. 11, 1902), No. 3872, p. 44.
69. *Dial,* XXXII (April 1, 1902), 248.
70. Henry Seton Merriman, *The Vultures* (New York and London, 1902).
71. *Athenaeum* (Sept. 20, 1902), No. 3908, p. 375.
72. *Academy,* LXIII (June–Dec., 1902), 215.
73. *Bookman* [American], XVII (Mar.–Aug., 1903), 101.
74. Oliver Edwards, *op. cit.*
75. According to a letter received in 1957 by Mrs. Olive D'Arcy Hart.
76. Henry Seton Merriman, *Barlasch of the Guard* (New York, 1903).
77. *Bookman* [English], XXV (Oct. 1903–Mar. 1904), 47–48.
78. *Athenaeum* (Aug. 29, 1903), No. 3957, p. 280.
79. *Academy,* LXV (July–Dec. 1903), 212.
80. Henry Seton Merriman, *The Last Hope* (New York, 1904).
81. *Bookman* [English], XXVII (Oct. 1904–Mar. 1905), 28.
82. *Academy,* LXVII (July–Dec. 1904), 197.
83. Oliver Edwards, *op. cit.*

Chapter Four

1. See footnote 58, Chapter 1.
2. This correspondence will be examined later in conjunction with a discussion of Merriman's short stories.
3. Henry Seton Merriman and Stephen G. Tallentyre, *From Wisdom Court* (London, 1893).

4. *Ibid.*, p. 76.
5. *Ibid.*, p. 81 ff.
6. *Ibid.*, pp. 150–51.
7. Henry Seton Merriman and S. G. Tallentyre, Preface, *The Money Spinner and Other Character Notes* (London, 1897).
8. *Academy*, LI (Jan.–June, 1897), 16.
9. *Cornhill* (New Series), I (July–Dec., 1896), 52, 361.
10. *Littell's Living Age*, CCX (Aug. 15, 1896), 446–48, and CCXI (Oct. 24, 1896), 206–10.
11. *McClure's*, VIII (Dec., 1896), 175–81.
12. *Ibid.*, p. 177.
13. *Idem.*
14. These letters were obtained from William Blackwood and Sons, Publishers, Edinburgh, through the good offices of Mrs. Olive S. D'Arcy Hart.
15. This information was conveyed in a letter of February 25, 1958, received from Mrs. Hart. See *Temple Bar*, CIX (Sept.–Dec., 1896), 396–404.
16. Henry Seton Merriman, *Tomaso's Fortune and Other Stories* (New York, 1904).
17. *Academy*, LXVI (Jan.–June, 1904), 521.
18. *Athenaeum* (May 14, 1904), No. 3994, p. 623.

Chapter Five

1. Oliver Edwards, *op. cit.*
2. Frank Swinnerton, *op. cit.*
3. Malcolm Elwin, *op. cit.*, p. 276.
4. *Ibid.*, p. 278.
5. *Outlook*, LXXV (Nov. 28, 1903), 723–24.
6. *Academy*, LXV (July–Dec., 1903), 577.
7. London *Times*, Nov. 20, 1903.
8. *Academy*, LII (July–Dec., 1897), 490.
9. Malcolm Elwin, *op. cit.*, p. 276.
10. Rudyard Kipling, *Kim* (New York, 1901), p. 452.
11. Lilias Rider Haggard, *The Cloak That I Left* (London, 1951), p. 118 ff.
12. Quoted by Lilias Rider Haggard, *op. cit.*, p. 258.
13. *Ibid.*, p. 128. Harold Williams, *Modern English Writers*, 3rd edition (London, 1925), p. 350.
14. Lilias Rider Haggard, *op. cit.*, p. 120.

Selected Bibliography

I. Primary Sources

1. *Books by Merriman* (*Editions referred to in text*)
Barlasch of the Guard. New York: McClure, Phillips and Co., 1903.
Dross. Chicago and New York: Herbert S. Stone, 1899.
Flotsam. New York: Longmans, Green, 1896.
From One Generation to Another. New York: Harper, 1893.
The Grey Lady. New York and London: Macmillan, 1895.
In Kedar's Tents. New York: New Amsterdam Book Co., 1903.
The Isle of Unrest. New York: Dodd, Mead, 1900.
The Last Hope. New York: Scribner's, 1904.
The Phantom Future. London: Smith, Elder, 1888.
Prisoners and Captives. New York: Dodd, Mead, 1899.
Roden's Corner. London: Smith, Elder, 1898.
The Slave of the Lamp. New York: F. M. Buckles and Co., 1903.
The Sowers. New York and London: Harper, 1899.
Suspense. New York: Dodd, Mead, 1899.
Tomaso's Fortune and Other Stories. New York: Scribner's, 1904.
The Velvet Glove. New York: Dodd, Mead, 1901.
The Vultures. New York and London: Harper, 1902.
With Edged Tools. New York: Harper, 1894.
Young Mistley. New York: A. Mackel and Co., 1899.

2. *Books by Merriman and Tallentyre*
From Wisdom Court. London: William Heinemann, 1893.
The Money Spinner and Other Character Notes. London: Smith, Elder, 1897.

3. *First Editions in England* (*arranged chronologically*)
Young Mistley. 2 vols. London: Bentley, 1888.
The Phantom Future. 2 vols. London: Bentley, 1888.
Suspense. 3 vols. London: Bentley, February, 1890.
Prisoners and Captives. 3 vols. London: Bentley, January, 1891.
The Slave of the Lamp. 2 vols. London: Smith, Elder, 1892.
From One Generation to Another. London: Smith, Elder, December, 1892.

(With Tallentyre, Stephen G.) *From Wisdom Court*. London: William Heinemann, 1893.

With Edged Tools. 2 vols. London: Smith, Elder, 1894.

The Grey Lady. London: Smith, Elder, 1895.

The Sowers. London: Smith, Elder, February, March, April, August, 1896.

Flotsam. London: Longman, July, 1896.

(With Tallentyre, S. G.) *The Money Spinner and Other Character Notes*. London: Smith, Elder, December, 1896.

In Kedar's Tents. London: Smith, Elder, October, 1897.

Roden's Corner. London: Smith, Elder, 1898.

Dross.* Chicago and New York: Herbert S. Stone, 1899.

The Isle of Unrest. London: Smith, Elder, 1899.

The Velvet Glove. London: Smith, Elder, December, 1901.

The Vultures. London: Smith, Elder, August, 1902.

Barlasch of the Guard. London: Smith, Elder, 1903.

Tomaso's Fortune and Other Stories. London: Smith, Elder, April, 1904.

The Last Hope. London: Smith, Elder, August, 1904.

4. Collected Edition

Scott, E. F. and Beatrice E. Hall, eds. *The Works of Henry Seton Merriman*. Memorial Edition, 14 vols. London: Smith, Elder, 1910. (Preface by E. F. Scott and "S. G. Tallentyre.") The only complete edition of Merriman's work, with a helpful preface by the author's widow and sister-in-law.

5. Partial List of Serial Publications

Bookman [American], VI (September, 1897–February, 1898). *In Kedar's Tents* serialized.

Cornhill, XVIII (January–June, 1892). *The Slave of the Lamp* serialized.

———— XXI, XXII (July, 1893–June, 1894). *With Edged Tools* serialized.

———— XXIV (January–June, 1895). *The Sowers* serialized.

———— (New Series). II and III (January–December, 1897). *In Kedar's Tents* serialized.

———— (New Series). VIII and IX (January–December, 1900). *The Isle of Unrest* serialized.

———— (New Series). XIV and XV (January–December, 1903). *Barlasch of the Guard* serialized.

---

* First edition of this book was published in America.

6. *Letters*

Butler, Patricia, A. P. Watt and Son, Literary Agents, Hastings House, 10 Norfolk Street, Strand, London, W.C. 2, England. (Letters to H. T. Cox, Philadelphia, Pa.) April 18, 1956; May 9, 1956; August 27, 1956.

Filon, S. P. L., Deputy Librarian, National Central Library, Malet Place, London, W.C. 1, England. (Letter to H. T. Cox, Philadelphia, Pa.) April 29, 1956.

Gibbs, Denise (Mrs.), Ampney St. Peter, near Cirencester, Gloucestershire. (Letter to H. T. Cox, Philadelphia, Pa.) October 14, 1956.

Greenall, D., Lloyd's, Information Department, London, E. C. 3, England. (Letter to Mrs. Olive S. D'Arcy Hart) January 16, 1957.

Hart, Olive S. D'Arcy (Mrs.), 21 Addison Avenue, Holland Park, London, W. 11, England. (Letters to H. T. Cox, Philadelphia, Pa.) December 30, 1956; January 19, 1957; January 30, 1957; April 1, 1957; April 27, 1957; July 20, 1957; September 8, 1957; October 14, 1957; November 17, 1957; February 25, 1958.

Hinkler, T., Treasury Chambers, Great George Street, London, S.W. 1, England. (Letter to Mrs. Olive S. D'Arcy Hart) January 9, 1957.

Hutchins, E. J., 31 Surrenden Crescent, Brighton, England. (Letter to H. T. Cox, Philadelphia, Pa.) April 28, 1957.

Jackson, J. G. Hamilton, Brigadoon, Buxted, Sussex. (Letters to Mrs. Olive S. D'Arcy Hart) January 25, 1957; January 29, 1957.

Murray, Sir John, Murray Publishers, Ltd., 50 Albemarle Street, London, W. 1, England. (Letter to Mrs. Olive S. D'Arcy Hart) January 8, 1957.

Rushton, Dorothy (Miss), 95 Bickenhall Mansions, London, W. 1, England. (Letter to Mrs. Olive S. D'Arcy Hart) January 29, 1957.

Scott, Hugh Stowell. (All letters to Wm. Blackwood Sons, Edinburgh, Scotland) Hooley Cottage, Merstham, Surrey, October 27, 1890; January 1, 1891; January 4, 1891; June 23, 1891; December 8, 1891; April 7, 1892; May 6, 1892; June 29, 1892; July 23, 1892; July 31, 1892; October 11, 1892; January 12, 1893; June 13, 1891. 27 Clements Lane, London, England, January 16, 1891; January 26, 1891. Hotel Bellevue, Menton, France, March 10, 1891.

———— Rome, Italy. (Letters to his mother) February 26, no year; March 3, no year. © 1956, Mrs. Denise Gibbs.

Spurr, Joseph, 22 Gilbert Road, Romford, Essex. (Letter to Mrs. Olive S. D'Arcy Hart) December 11, 1956.

Swinnerton, Frank, Old Tokefield, Cranleigh, Surrey. (Letter to H. T. Cox, Philadelphia, Pa.) August 28, 1956.

Webb, Richard E., British Information Services, 45 Rockefeller Plaza,

New York 20, N.Y. (Letter to H. T. Cox, Philadelphia, Pa.) April 1, 1957.

7. Unpublished Material

Certificate of Birth (No. 329219). General Register Office, Somerset House, London, England.

Certificate of Death (No. 203883). General Register Office, Somerset House, London, England.

Maggs Brothers, Messrs. Booksellers, Berkeley Square, London, England. (Excerpt from Maggs' catalogue containing a long quotation from Scott's letter to his mother [dated Fecamp, June 7, 1895] in which he reveals his identity as Henry Seton Merriman.)

Scott, Hugh Stowell. Diary of a voyage to Madras, Calcutta, Ceylon, Aden, Gibraltar, and return to Southampton, 1877–1878. Unpublished manuscript. © 1956, Mrs. Denise Gibbs.

———— Last Will and Testament (with codicils). October 14, 1896.

Williams, the Rev. G. "The Wisdom of Henry Seton Merriman." Unpublished collection of memorabilia compiled for private circulation.

II. Selected Secondary Sources

1. Books Referring to Merriman

Baker, Ernest A. *A Guide to Historical Fiction*. London: George Routledge and Sons, 1914. Lists authors and titles of historical fiction, with brief summarizing sentences about each book.

———— and James Packman. *A Guide to the Best Fiction*. New York: Macmillan, 1929. An expansion of Prof. Baker's *Guide to Historical Fiction*.

Bateson, F. W., ed. *Cambridge Bibliography of English Literature*. Vol. III. New York: Macmillan, 1941. A valuable source for checking dates of first editions, etc.

Cumulative Index. Cleveland, Ohio: The Public Library. Also useful for establishing first edition dates.

Elwin, Malcolm. *Old Gods Falling*. New York: Macmillan, 1939. Contains one of the most extensive treatments of Merriman; but this treatment, perceptive as it is, extends only to a couple of pages.

English Catalogue of Books, The. Vols. IV, V, VI. London: Sampson, Low, Marston and Co. Helpful in establishing first issue dates.

Gissing, George. *Veranilda*. New York: Dutton, 1905. Interesting basis of comparison for Merriman's historical fiction.

Haggard, Lilias Rider. *The Cloak That I Left*. London: Hodder and

Stoughton, 1951. Furnishes a basis of comparison for Merriman's techniques.

KENNEDY, J. M. *English Literature, 1880–1905.* London: Stephen Swift and Co., 1912. Contains brief mention of Merriman.

KIPLING, RUDYARD. *Kim.* New York: Doubleday, Page and Co., 1901. A basis of comparison for Merriman's use of theme.

KUNITZ, STANLEY J. and HOWARD HAYCRAFT. *British Authors of the Nineteenth Century.* New York: H. H. Wilson, 1936. A good, but brief, notice of Merriman and his work.

LEE, SIR SIDNEY, ED. *Dictionary of National Biography.* Vol. III. London: Smith, Elder, 1912. Brief biographical notice on Merriman.

SADLEIR, MICHAEL. *XIX Century Fiction.* Vol. 1 of 2 vols. Cambridge University Press, 1951. Among others, lists Merriman's works with publication dates.

SOMERVELL, D. C. *English Thought in the Nineteenth Century.* New York: Longmans, Green, 1926. An excellent volume on the philosophical backgrounds of the nineteenth century.

VILLIERS, FREDERIC. *Villiers: His Five Decades of Adventure.* Vol. II. New York and London: Harper, 1920. A fascinating account by a gentleman adventurer who was acquainted with a great many famous men of his time; a portion of one chapter deals with a visit paid to the Scott home when young Hugh was in his teens.

WAGENKNECHT, EDWARD. *Cavalcade of the English Novel.* New York: Century, 1954. Wagenknecht gives a brief paragraph to Merriman in the appendix to this volume.

WEYGANDT, CORNELIUS. *A Century of the English Novel.* New York: Century, 1925. An excellent study of the novel, but with scant mention of Merriman.

WEYMAN, STANLEY J. *Under the Red Robe.* In the volume *Historical Romances.* New York: Longmans, Green and Co., 1921. Shows the divergence of techniques in respect to the historical novel existing between Merriman and his long-time friend.

Who Was Who. London: A. and C. Black, 1920. Brief but helpful biographical data.

WILLIAMS, HAROLD. *Modern English Writers: Being a Study of Imaginative Literature, 1890–1914.* London: Sidgwick and Jackson, 3rd edition, 1925. Although he omits Merriman, Mr. Williams' comments on this author's contemporaries are illuminating.

YOUNG, G. M. *Victorian England: Portrait of an Age.* New York: Doubleday and Co., 1954. One of the most helpful books written on the spirit of Victorians and Victorianism.

2. *Periodicals—Reviews of Merriman's Work*

Academy, XXXIII (February 4, 1888), 76.
——— XXXVII (January–June, 1890), 166.
——— XXXIX (March 7, 1891), 230.
——— XLIX (January–June, 1896), 320.
——— L (July–December, 1896), 257–58.
——— LI (January–June, 1897), 16.
——— LII (July–December, 1897), 359, 490.
——— LIV–LV (July–December, 1898), 296.
——— LIX (July–December, 1900), 242, 416.
——— LXI (July–December, 1901), 171.
——— LXIII (July–December, 1902), 215.
——— LXV (July–December, 1903), 212, 577, 579.
——— LXVI (January–June, 1904), 521.
——— LXVII (July–December, 1904), 197.

Athenaeum (March 9, 1889), No. 3202, p. 309.
——— (April 12, 1890), No. 3259, p. 467.
——— (February 14, 1891), No. 3303, p. 214.
——— (May 7, 1892), No. 3367, p. 599.
——— (March 25, 1893), No. 3413, p. 373.
——— (September 2, 1893), No. 3436, p. 321.
——— (January 11, 1896), No. 3559, p. 50.
——— (March 14, 1896), No. 3568, p. 341.
——— (November 6, 1897), No. 3654, p. 629.
——— (September 29, 1900), No. 3805, p. 408.
——— (January 11, 1903), No. 3872, p. 44.
——— (May 14, 1904), No. 3994, p. 623.

Bookman [American], III (February, 1896), 56–57.
——— XII (September, 1900–February, 1901), 584.
———XVII (March–August, 1903), 101.

Bookman [English], III (October, 1892–March, 1893), 130.
——— XIII (October, 1897–March, 1898), 105–6.
———XV (October, 1898–March, 1899), 20–21.
——— XIX (October, 1900–March, 1901), 61.
——— XXV (October, 1903–March, 1904), 47–48.
——— XXVII (October, 1904–March, 1905), 28.

Cornhill (New Series), I (July–December, 1896), 52, 361.

Critic, XXVII (April 10, 1895), 254.
——— XXVIII (February 8, 1896), 93.

Dial, XXIII (December 16, 1893), 391.
——— XXV (December 16, 1898), 457.
——— XXXII (April 1, 1902), 248.

Selected Bibliography

Edwards, Oliver. "The Sense of Duty," London *Times* (October 3, 1957).

Harper's, XCVII (October, 1898), Fourth Supplement.

Harper's Bazaar, XXXI, 948.

Illustrated American, XXIII, 57.

Illustrated London News, CXIII, 312.

Literary Weekly, XXVII (March 12, 1896), 92.

———— XXIX (June 11, 1898), 183.

———— XXX (May 27, 1899), 163.

Littell's Living Age, CCX (August 15, 1896), 446–48.

———— CCXI (October 24, 1896), 206–10.

London *Times,* "Henry Seton Merriman." Obituary. (November 20, 1903).

McClure's, VIII (December, 1896), 175–81.

Monthly Review, XVII (No. 1), 168.

Outlook, LX (November 12, 1898), 677.

———— LXXV (November 28, 1903), 723–24.

Saturday Review, LXXXII (August 22, 1896), 191.

———— LXXXIV (October 30, 1897), 474.

Swinnerton, Frank. "Master of Romance," *John O'London's Weekly,* LX (December 14, 1951), 881.

Index